SOUL MAGIC

Understanding Your Journey

Other Titles From New Falcon Publications

The Tree of Life—Paths in Jungian Individuation
Buddhism and Jungian Psychology
By J. Marvin Spiegelman, Ph.D.
Cosmic Trigger: The Final Secret of the Illuminati
Prometheus Rising
By Robert Anton Wilson
Undoing Yourself With Energized Meditation
Secrets of Western Tantra
By Christopher S. Hyatt, Ph.D.
Eight Lectures on Yoga
Gems From the Equinox
The Pathworkings of Aleister Crowley
By Aleister Crowley
Neuropolitique
Info-Psychology
The Game of Life
By Timothy Leary, Ph.D.
Zen Without Zen Masters
By Camden Benares
Condensed Chaos: An Introduction to Chaos Magick
By Phil Hine
Breaking the Godspell
By Neil Freer
The Complete Golden Dawn System of Magic
The Golden Dawn Tapes—Series I, II, and III
By Israel Regardie
Astrology & Consciousness: The Wheel of Light
By Rio Olesky
Metaskills: The Spiritual Art of Therapy
By Amy Mindell, Ph.D.
The Mysteries Revealed
By Andrew Schneider
Beyond Duality: The Art of Transcendence
By Laurence Galian
Carl Sagan & Immanuel Velikovsky
By Charles Ginenthal

And to get your free catalog of *all* of our titles, write to:

New Falcon Publications (Catalog Dept.)
1739 East Broadway Road, Suite 1-277
Tempe, Arizona 85282 U.S.A

SOUL MAGIC

Understanding Your Journey

By
Katherine Torres, Ph.D.

Illustrated by
Pam Posey

1995
NEW FALCON PUBLICATIONS
TEMPE, ARIZONA, U.S.A.

International Standard Book Number: 1-56184-077-7

First Edition 1995

Illustrations by Pam Posey
Cover by S. Jason Black

The paper used in this publication meets the minimum requirements of the American National Standard for Permanence of Paper for Printed Library Materials Z39.48-1984

Address all inquiries to:
NEW FALCON PUBLICATIONS
1739 East Broadway Road Suite 1-277
Tempe, AZ 85282 U.S.A.
(or)
1605 East Charleston Blvd.
Las Vegas, NV 89104 U.S.A.

Dedicated to
Soul Searchers Throughout the World

THE UNIVERSE IS INTELLIGENT
THE SOUL IS AN ASPECT OF THE UNIVERSE
THE SOUL IS INTELLIGENT

ACKNOWLEDGMENTS

It is always a delight to say thank you to those who help you on your pathway. This book would not have come together without clients and friends and I want to thank them all. Alas, there is not enough room.

However, special acknowledgment is due the people who allowed me to put their Sacred Path Wheels© into this volume of information. First, thanks to Diane McPherson. She has allowed me to reveal herself to the whole world. You will get to know her well. Earl Beam offered his wheel, and any other help he could provide. Bobbie Wilson consented to let me use her life-time information without a second thought. To you all I say thank you and appreciate your gift and trust.

My good friend and companion Suzanne Merritt-Palka was a guinea pig for me. She allowed herself to be the first to experience the Sacred Path Wheel©. Lee Tollefson also stepped in at the beginning and asked to have a chart done. These dear friends were willing to let me "start" this venture of charting through their sacred energy.

I owe an exceptional thanks to two very dear friends and supporters, Judy and Ron Keeler. They not only had personal wheels done, but they went on to make sure everyone in their family knew their path, and then they had a wheel done that revealed the path of their relationship. Also, without hesitation they supported the finish of this project. I am delighted to say, "It's here!" Thank you both.

Throughout the book are several delightful illustrations and Pam Posey is to be thanked for her imaginative art work. Thanks Pam.

I could not go without thanking my publisher/editor, Nick Tharcher. I had such fun and enjoyment working with him. Nick, you're great and thanks for putting this work together. It's been exciting.

And Eva Shaw—Thank you so much for seeing a book potential from my dissertation. Without your suggestions this may have simply stayed in the Westbrook archives.

I certainly wish to acknowledge my always patient and loving husband, Al. During the years of preparing this book he ignored the hours of separation, the constant clutter around the house, dinners alone, and the lack of clear communication when we did have time together. I love you Al and thank you for your complete support.

This book has been a work of love and insight and I am grateful for the opportunity to share it.

TABLE OF CONTENTS

FIGURES

TABLES

INTRODUCTION

Soul Magic—What Is It?

Shrouded in mystery, soundlessly expressing, and deeply felt is the soul. It is the intangible quality of our immortal self. We experience *soul* in many things. Immersed in personal thought we are soul-full. Listening to music we hear soul. Singers have soul. Engrossed in a book we connect with soul. Writers write with soul.

Daily the soul exists within and around us. It leads us on our journey, allows us to explore the many facets of the day and provides us with necessary survival instincts. This survival is magical, miraculous, and seemingly purposeful. Something within driving us to be, act, achieve and experience everything before us. What is this drive? Is it magic? Is it the soul? What is "soul" and does it have a purpose?

Today we search for greater meaning of ourselves. We wonder what lies beyond materialism. We ask how we can connect to our spirituality. We want to know how to connect more deeply and meaningfully to the people in our lives and the world in which we live. In other words, we want to know how to connect with our soul-self and our greater reason for being.

It has been my utmost joy and pleasure to search for the mystical treasures of the Universe. Many pathways have crossed my corridors. At times I join these pathways and traverse their wisdom-trails. Along the trails I discover archetypes and symbols of a soul's journey. The symbols contain a map-like language and provide a delightful way to share the jewels of the Universe. The symbols contain an explanation of the soul and its magic.

Imagine, if you will, a realm of nonphysical existence just before birth. It is a time of preparation to enter the land of Earth. You are in communication with God, angels and other soul brothers and sisters. You are talking about your plans for the journey into a physical life. You have a mission and a desire to fulfill a goal, and you want help. You want support from guardians from the spiritual realm. You want to be instinctually strong so you can survive in a realm of unknowns.

Adaptation and growth is a requirement for this journey. Self expression will be important. Personal power is to be explored. Interaction with others is essential. Intuition will help you move through this journey with an inner knowing when the knowing seems impossible. You will want to assist others and gift your talents to help humanity. You will want to connect to the Light of God/Goddess and express it through the spectrum of colors. These are your plans and you are asking for help.

Those in the meeting are supportive. Some offer their assistance as interpersonal relationships on the land of Earth. Guardian angels offer support to inspire and protect you. God offers much more—*all* of the energies of the Universe. The stars and planets will be provided as emanations of energies expressing as your personality. Frequencies of the plants, animals and minerals will be transformed through you as energies of growth, instinct, and a foundation on which to perform your lesson. Light frequencies will pour forth through the spectrum of the Universe and offer you healing, personal power, and manifesting abilities for all that you require. Your very name will provide an energetic pattern for helping you express and fulfill your journey. You accept the help. As you pull it all together and work with others the plan for your Earth existence is set in motion. The journey of your soul begins. You decide to leap into the physical realm.

Entering the land of Earth creates the longing to understand your purpose, your soul, and the Universe. One cycle leads to the next. The desire to understand reaches into the recesses of antiquity. It stems from the question asked by every human being: Who am I? Suffice it to say, all religions and spiritual beliefs delegate the soul as a product of a higher being, God, the Creator of all life. God is an intelligent being and holds this world and Universe in a regulated state of order. From the intelligence of this Creator, life forms are conceived and include the existence of human beings housing a soul.

Human beings are given the high esteem of being on a par to God. The first book of the Bible, Genesis 2:27, states, "So God created man in his *own image*, in the image of God he created him; male and female he created them." (Emphasis mine.) This image is the soul while God is the Spirit. Ernest Holmes points out that "There is a Universal Mind, Spirit, Intelligence, that is the origin of everything: It is First Cause or God" (1966:81). He declares that the soul is the medium through which the Spirit operates (1966:90); for "It is the business of the Soul to reflect the images that Spirit casts into It." (1966:91)

Philosophers throughout history have contemplated this essence and intelligence called the "soul." Socrates, the Greek philosopher, often theorized about the nature of the soul, personal intelligence, and its origin. During the last days of his life he was consumed with the need to understand soul existence and personal intelligence. Throughout a long conversation with his friend and companion, Simmias, he speculated about this question of intelligence, how one exists and experiences life. On the day of his death, he finally presented an answer. He concluded that knowledge resides in the soul and is recollected from the soul, and that the soul of each person "...were possessed of intelligence." (Tredennick, 1982:126). Is intelligence the magic? Is that what leads us through a lifetime?

As we sojourn through the world of spiritual and philosophical beliefs repeated questions do occur. How do we prove this intelligence? What will it serve? Many agree that intelligence does exist. Yet can we, in the world of matter, prove this intelligence? If we know this information, will it help us live a more joyous and forward-moving existence?

Looking over a person's life we can recognize an intelligence at work. First this intelligence survives the onrush of life from conception through the birth canal. Then the journey through childhood takes the personality into training and preparation for adulthood. Each person is unique even within a family framework of conditioning. Each person seems to have a drive to be something, do something significant, and accomplish a great goal in their life. Individuals ask "What is it I am to do?" This question is deeply felt and spiritually motivated. As though each individual is asking God, "Why did you put me here?" Or, asking their soul, "What is my purpose?"

For over thirty years I have considered these questions. Throughout the past decade, I have been involved in the study of the existence of the soul, its intelligence and if it has a purpose as it lives through any given lifetime. This study came about because of my own spiritual convictions and desire to know what I am to do. Especially if I am to achieve something for the "good of my soul" or for the creator of all life, God. I have researched for me and for many clients and students. I have studied religions of the world, other philosophers' understanding of the soul, and finally I have studied through deep meditation.

A process known as channeling became an avenue for understanding and charting the soul, its intelligence, its journey, and its magic. Channeling, as Jon Klimo explains, is "the communication of information to or through a physically embodied human being from a source that is said to exist on some other level or dimension of reality than the physical as we know it..." (1987:2). I prefer to call it a method of communicating with the Higher Intelligence of the Universe. Most particularly, it came through the process and connection I have with a spiritual being, whom I call Malachi, my guardian angel. For several years Malachi has been providing me with information that is Universal and can be applied as guidance for daily living. During many sessions in communication with Malachi he also provided information for others and ways in which individuals can enhance their understanding of life on a personal level. Malachi has lead me to study methods of understanding the Universe through exploration of ancient cultures and information provided by ancestors of humanity. My adventures in ancestral studies took me on a path of Native American and Celtic review. Both cultures use a circle for gathering and connecting with spiritual consciousness. Both cultures use the circle as a way to follow the cycles of life. I began teaching a class in Native traditions that allowed students to follow a year-long path for personal unfoldment through a medicine wheel. During a day of class preparation, Malachi entered my focus of attention. He expressed a way in which the wheel could be used to interpret the journey of a soul through a lifetime. The journey, he noted, is an achievement of a Life Lesson. Malachi also informed me that I could reach into the pathways of an individual's life through meditation and channeling. This suggested that I could provide guidance to an individual so they could enhance their ability to learn their life lesson. In the following chapters the methods used for interpreting information provided through channeling will be given.

Using channeling as a method of study and exploration revealed exciting journeys into the intelligence or "magic" of the soul. While delving into the psyche of individuals, it became apparent that the soul creates goals for learning and growing in each incarnation. The soul explores many facets of the Universe with a need to be whole and one with its true spiritual nature—God. It has a natural desire to move to wholeness. It has an inherent motivator provided by God, the Creator. The soul acts in an individualized manner experiencing events which places it on a course toward perfection. The state of perfection is Oneness with God. The soul journeys through one life after another gathering experiences and knowledge. Each lifetime assists the soul in its return to Oneness and its full intelligence as God.

The soul does indeed have a purpose. It intends to achieve knowledge and learn about all states of existence. It intends to learn lessons as it traverses one century after another. Each lifetime it has a particular lesson to learn and will access many energetic patterns to assist the journey toward completion of the lesson.

As I travel the spiritual patterns of individuals, I observe the energies that assist the lessons. These energies incorporate instinctual and intuitive awareness, unique expressions of self and electromagnetic colors that enhance it all. Spiritual assistants consistently support the journey. They present guidance on the pathway of life. The energies are also connected to the cosmos, animals, plants, and minerals. These energies are easily associated with the soft sciences of metaphysics: Astrology, Qabalah, numerology, mythology, and others. Using various metaphysical correspondences a charting system and a proving ground for revealing the true magic of the soul has been developed.

Charting Soul Magic

For several years I have been plotting charts (Figure 1-1) for individuals that have led them to understand themselves more clearly and to understand their *Life Lesson.* This comprehension has helped them be more alert and attentive to their purpose for incarnating.

Creating the charts has also helped me in following the edict of Hermes Trismegistus. Hermes requested that a student study the Universe, verify the studies, understand and incorporate the information provided and only then believe what has been received. This I did and fully came to the place of admiration. I was awe-inspired by the soul and its magic.

As I charted the information received, a method of deciphering the unseen realities of the Universe was translated into a language usable by the human thinking process. I noted the language of God is presented to humanity as symbolism (stars and planets, mountains and lakes, crosses and circles, and so forth). Symbolism is also the manner in which humanity attempts to explain the Universe. Therefore, symbolism became the common ground for explaining the seen and unseen realities in my charting system. Once a language of correspondences was established, the whys and wherefores of existence simply fell into my sphere of knowledge.

In the realm of metaphysics today many deciphering methods exist. As we venture through the wheel of soul magic throughout this book, the tools used to correlate the energy of the Universe to the intelligence of the soul will be reviewed. An individual chart will be explored in this book to provide you with a deeper understanding of the relationship everyone has to this vast Universe and the intelligence that maintains the order of our existence.

The chart developed to interpret the intelligence of the soul is known as the Sacred Path Wheel©. It is a 12-spoke circle. As seen from the titles within each spoke (Figure 1-1), the chart provides information about the life lesson of a person, their spiritual guardian, their identity as seen in their name, their instinctual nature, growth nature, and so on. When tied together there is a whole picture of the soul-process for incarnating and achieving a goal within a particular lifetime. This goal is the achievement of a life lesson. The wheel provides an understanding of the Universal energies used to create a whole person, personality traits, and other Universal expressions to support a lifetime process.

This book will take you on a journey to understand soul magic. It will show you how each person, through the agency of their soul, connects to the supporting elements of the Universe. Then, through a conduit it enters the land of Earth and participates in the magical theater of life. As you will see, the soul is magical, intelligent and awesome.

Each chapter will provide you an opportunity to explore your own soul intelligence. Discover the magic through meditation. Keep a journal. By the time you finish this book you will have created your very own Sacred Path Wheel and will be able to be inspired by the intelligence of your soul. This knowledge will encourage you to be conscious of the steps you take every day to achieve the goal of your soul in this incarnation.

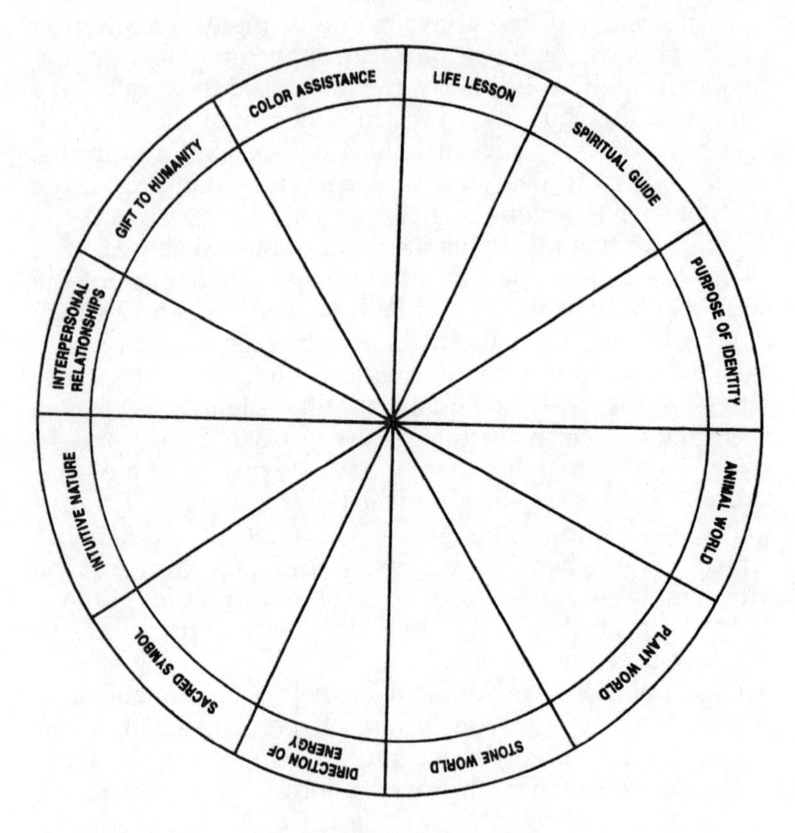

Figure 1-1
Sacred Path Wheel©

Creating Your Sacred Space

If you want to create your own Sacred Path Wheel, then before starting on your journey it is important to prepare a sacred place for your meditation time. Find a spot in your house or out in nature. Let it be a place that is both private and easy to access. Create an altar that will inspire you to relax and move into an altered state of consciousness. Put items on your altar that are important to you, such as your journal, inspirational pictures, crystals, or statues. Include two candles. Place one on the left that will represent your inner consciousness where you connect with the God/ Goddess of All Creation. Let the right candle represent your outer consciousness where you bring to your own attention that which you learn on your journey. Light the left candle first. Then light the right candle. Create a prayer statement each time you meditate. Ask for assistance from the Great Spirit and the guardians of the Sacred Path Wheel.

Each chapter has a guided meditation prepared to take you through the portals of the wheel. You may want to record the meditation on a cassette so you may relax and be guided. Once you have received your information, jot it down in your journal. When you have received insight for all twelve spokes, then you will want to create a wheel. In each spoke simply write one sentence for its meaning. Where you can, place a picture. For instance, an angel can be placed in the Spiritual Guardian spoke. Pictures of your animal, plant and mineral are appropriate. Drawing your symbol is helpful in reminding you of the law or laws you are to be aware of.

With this information at hand, you can enliven your pathway and stay on course.

If you prefer to have someone else prepare your Sacred Path Wheel you will find an order blank at the end of the book. I will be delighted to connect with your energy and the guardians of the wheel to discover your sacred path.

CHAPTER 2

Purpose of Incarnation

At birth the curtains open to the theater of life. Though a baby seems fragile and innocent, wisdom abounds in the child's soul. It knows why it is here and what it must do. Throughout its physical lifetime it will appear as though this knowledge is hidden. The truth is, however, the knowledge is always available and being uncovered with every step taken in life.

Life Lesson

Each individual enters life with a purpose. This purpose is to learn a *Life* lesson. The intention is to grow and learn about a certain aspect of the greater whole. By living out a life lesson, soul evolution is achieved. A life lesson isn't necessarily something to be done for the world at large. It may not even be leadership for humanity (like the president of a country, or a major spiritual leader). This learning may simply be how to relate to others or how to own your own power. A life lesson is often a personal growth aspect—learning about yourself. For instance, in my last incarnation I was the mother of four children and the wife of a rancher. I worked very hard each and every day. I tended my family by cooking, canning, making their clothes, taking care of the general area around the ranch house, and from my garden I created remedies for whatever healing purposes we needed, and also the food to sustain us. I lived a rugged life. My husband was gone most of the time as he tended the acreage of our vast land. At the time of my death I reviewed my life and discovered that I had learned what it meant to work hard. I said to myself, "I didn't need to work so hard." I came through the education of life that taught me what hard work provided. I vowed to balance that reality when entering this incarnation. As I began my adult life this time around I came very close to repeating the same pattern. I had four children, I cooked, canned, made their clothes, and worked very hard. My husband was gone most of the time. Somewhere along the way an inner voice whispered, "You do not have to work so hard. This is not God's intention." I began to challenge myself and change my reality. When I balance through this incarnation I will have completed a polarity package of hard work/not working so hard. I will realize that the essence I call God is the worker, not the personality I call myself. I will be able to take this information, store it within my soul memory bank and move onto another adventure and study of the Divine.

Balance is called *Karma*—The Law of Cause and Effect. To obtain balance the soul journeys through lifetimes. The search is always to know the whole by living its parts. One lifetime may include peace and harmony while the next may bring about the understanding of struggle and fear. One lifetime may be the experience of total health while another may be the experience of constant physical illness. Each lifetime is balancing the other and providing knowledge of both sides of the scale.

When a soul chooses to enter the Earth school it does so with the intent to learn something of importance. It may be to balance the scale from a lifetime already explored. It may be the opportunity to begin a journey into something totally different and process one side of the scale, leaving another lifetime for the opposite side of the scale to be discovered. Always the desire is to explore "one more aspect" of the vast creation of all life.

This innate drive of the soul is so strong that the personality "feels" it throughout its life. Sometimes that feeling is an unexplainable urge to do something important, to serve humanity, and to know more about this

Universe. In whatever manner the feeling surfaces, the individual knows s/he must accomplish this great desire. The feeling always encourages the question, "What is my purpose?" The soul carries an encoded message to "advance at all costs toward perfection and union with the whole." This message urges the soul to evolve through lifetimes and lessons. These lessons become the ultimate drive of the soul as it personifies the drama of living within the auditorium of life.

As I explore the life lessons of individuals through the Sacred Path Wheel charting system, I discover that the intention to learn the Life Lesson is well ingrained within the soul. Many aspects of an incarnation are to be experienced in order to carry out this mission. Before birth the soul pulls together all the energies available to assist the Life Lesson. The Guardians, the name to be utilized as the personality, the instinctual nature, and so on, are chosen to assist in the purpose of learning the Life Lesson. Repeatedly it has been revealed that each person connects with a variety of supporting energies within the Universe.

Throughout the channeling, study, and evaluation of Sacred Path Wheels the continual review of the soul intelligence proves to be awe-inspiring. The findings, incredibly, reveal choices that cannot be denied as anything else but soul intelligence. As this narrative continues, the wheel of a client will be utilized to explore the awesome intelligence and magic of the soul (Figure 2-1). This review and evaluation will enable you to obtain an understanding of the Universe in its intelligent emanation through a soul and acted out by a personality. It most certainly will reveal the repeated awareness of the soul as it aligns with choices to follow particular patterns of growth.

Diane's Life Lesson

Diane McPherson is a client, student, friend and teacher. She was born in the month of March under the sign of Aries. The moon was in Sagittarius and she had dual rising signs, Gemini and Cancer. Upon receiving her Sacred Path Wheel her life was changed. She awakened to a truth within herself that has helped her "take charge" of her life and walk a knowing path rather than be frightened by a hidden purpose. Diane has graciously allowed me to include her chart information. It will help you understand the power and knowing of the soul magic that exists within each one of us.

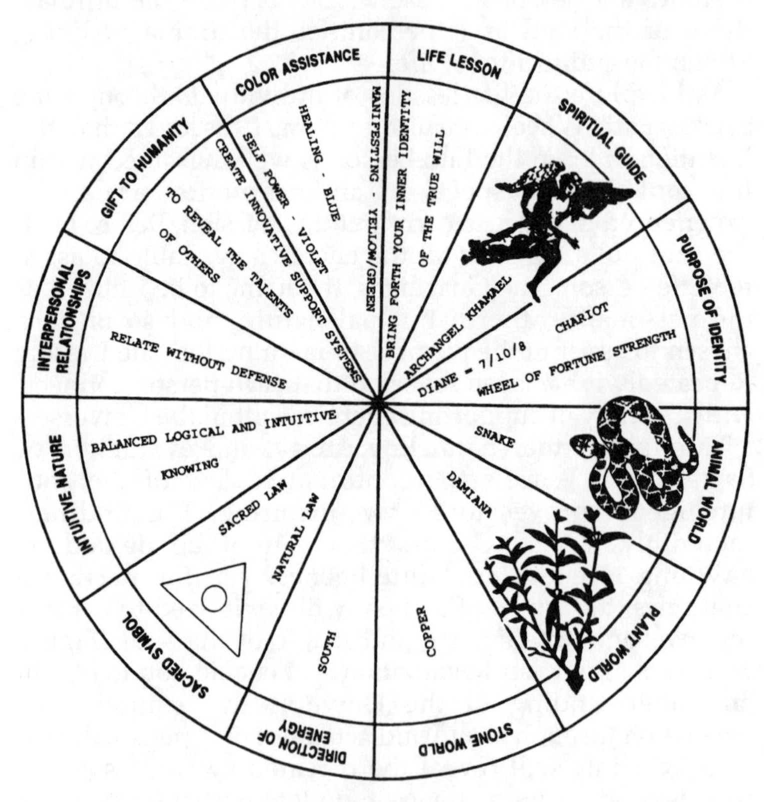

Figure 2-1
Diane McPherson's Sacred Path Wheel©

As I entered the space of meditation and connected to Diane's inner knowledge, her Life Lesson was revealed (Figure 2-2). It was clearly a goal for bringing forth her inner identity throughout this Earth journey.

True to form, Diane works on this constantly. That is the way it is for all of us. We work with both the positive and challenging aspects of our purpose.

As you move through this book you will see how Diane's soul chose circumstances and energy patterns to help her accomplish her goal. Also true to form, it is a joy as well as a challenge for Diane to work with her blueprint.

The soul creates challenges so the individual will not become complacent. Complacency creates inactivity and the purpose of evolution is not accomplished if the individual is without drive toward a goal.

Action toward achieving a goal, with conscious awareness of our activities and interpersonal relationships, helps us master our Life Lesson. If we choose to ignore our pathway, our soul will stir up a challenge to bring us to awareness. As you can see, a general discussion of Diane's life lesson is provided. Challenges are also revealed as indicators of when Diane needs to be prodded toward her ultimate goal and removed from a state of complacency. Also, when awakened by the prodding, a way out of the challenge can be used to set her back on track and into balance.

Lesson: *Bring forth your inner identity.* Your inner identity is your True Will and is to be activated and identified by you through this physical journey. It is strong, powerful and successful. It is activated by knowing yourself and acting from that nature. You activate it by being clear, coming from your space of inner power, and manifesting your inner dreams. Empowerment is experienced by you through integrity, strength, the balance of spirit and mind, and the manifestation of your inner-most desires.
Challenge: You will be in negative experiences of your life lesson when you 1) allow others to force their will upon you, 2) you force your will upon others, 3) you do not fulfill your dreams, 4) you allow a misalignment with spirit and mind, and 5) you become complacent or inactive. All of this will negate your inner identity—your True Will. You will experience strife, struggle, and an inability to manifest your inner-most dreams. Your passion will be a fantasy. Your spiritual and mental realities will be out of balance.
Way Out: Connect with your inner forces. Feel the power of your core self—your True Will. Then act upon it. Be it. Empower yourself from the space of your inner knowing. Be focused in thought and spirit. Become vocal with your desires—name your power. Name your True Will. Bring it out into the world of form. Stand up for who you are with strength, integrity, and mastery. Own your power.

Figure 2-2
Diane McPherson's Life Lesson

Discovering Your Life Lesson

The secret of your purpose lies within you. Knowing your life lesson will aid you in making sound decisions toward the advancement of your soul-evolution. Being in tune with your life lesson will lift your spirit and gift you with a sense of joy, direction, and accomplishment.

Set your altar, particularly if you have created a portable one. If you have candles, light the one on the left first to stir the knowledge from within and activate your Higher Mind. Then, light the right candle to signify that your conscious mind will be aware and receptive to the knowledge presented by your Higher Mind.

Take a few moments to create a quiet space of inner reflection. Ask that the higher consciousness within you be your guide. Drift into a meditation by imagining a forest before you. Walk through the forest and ask to be taken to a sacred place, the inner spaces of your soul. When you feel connected to this place, ask your higher consciousness to reveal your purpose for being here. Allow the knowledge of your Life Lesson to be revealed through feeling, thought, and vision. When you return from your quiet place of meditation, write your message down in a journal. Contemplate on this Life Lesson. How have you been acting upon it throughout this life? How can you consciously assist yourself to achieve this lesson? Observe yourself over the next few days to see how this lesson gets played out in your every day interactions.

CHAPTER 3

Wings of Support

Spirit Guardian

Angels are indeed aspects of this vast Universe. They are the supporters of the souls traversing the Earth. They are assistants of the One Great Spirit. They are guardians of the sacred energies of the Divine.

Angels know that as each soul enters the birth canal a darkness occurs. The shadow of consciousness becomes evident as the soul leaves the sphere of Spirit and begins to explore the Earth. The initial alignment with Earth is an apparent separation from the Great Creator. The personality begins to experience a sense of aloneness. The personal body encapsulates energies of the mind, emotions, and spirit. Each of these levels of the individual is contained within itself. However, the experience of containment is one of loneliness and separateness, creating a lack of understanding ones connection with the Universe, other people, and circumstances. Oh, but for the grace of angels.

No one enters this Earth alone though it may seem so. Each soul is guided by spiritual support. Though there are many spiritual beings who can assist a person through their passage, there is one particular being who is the overseer. This guardian is entrusted with ministering to the personality encapsulated in a body. This spiritual being is related to the Guardian Angels of Christian, Judeo, and Islamic philosophies. The focus in the Sacred Path Wheel©

is on the archetypal world of Archangels, and Orders of Angels.

Malachi, my guardian, instructs me to connect with the ten major Archangels and the Order of Angels that support them in order to obtain the true guardianship of an individual. He informs me that there are many guardians in the heavens and many will be and can be experienced by a person. However, it is at the level of the Archangels and the Order of Angels that the overseer occurs. It is this angelic being that is called forward to make sure the person hears, feels, and knows the call of his/her soul purpose.

The role of the Angels has been discussed and contemplated at great length for centuries. One of the greatest systems for utilizing and connecting with the Angels is the study of the Tree of Life. Most often, this study is through the ancient Jewish mystical system called Qabalah. It has been dispersed through the mystical schools of western philosophy as well. The Tree of Life philosophy provides a map of creation as related to the plans of the Divine Mind.

During my meditational process for receiving life data for an individual an angelic guide is revealed. The guide may appear to me in spheres of lights and colors, through angelic-looking forms, or through thought impressions. The angel or archangel, who is the ultimate guardian of the soul purpose, is related to one of the ten spheres of consciousness known on the Tree of Life. As research of the Tree of Life reveals, each angel has a particular manner for assisting. The assistance can be related to an emanation of color, a planet, and certainly to a particular aspect of developing consciousness. (William G. Gray, 1987). Through understanding the angel and the assistance he can provide, an association can be made as to why the soul has chosen this particular guardian.

Table 3-1 is a chart of the ten superior angels—known as Archangels—and their compatriots, the Order of Angels. A simple description of correspondences is also noted.

In researching Diane's wheel we see by the discussion of Diane's Spiritual Guardian, (Figure 3-1) why her soul chose the overseer who would most powerfully enhance her inner impulse to go forward with the goal of her soul. Of interest is the fact that Diane was born under the sign of Aries. This zodiacal sign is ruled by the planet Mars. Khamael, her guardian, is the ruler of Mars. (Similar notes of interest were found in several charts I delineated. In one way or another, confirmation occurred to support astrological alignment as another component of the soul choosing a myriad of Universal energies to augment association with a soul purpose.) Khamael also oversees the sphere of Divine Consciousness that sets in motion the intent to "move forward at all costs." This energy will always push Diane forward and not allow her to stay in the challenge for a great length of time.

Archangel	Order of Angels	Correspondence on the Tree of Life
Metatron	Holy Living Creatures	Focus, Beginning
Ratziel	Auphanim	Wisdom, knowledge
Tzaphkiel	Aralim	Understanding, Boundaries, One as Many
Tzadkiel	Chasmalim	Inspiration, Benevolence
Khamael	Seraphim	Severity, Courage, Change
Michael	Malachim	Love, Balance, Self
Haniel	Elohim	Desire, Valor, Endurance
Raphael	Beni Elohim	Intelligence, Splendor
Gabriel	Kerubim	Reproduction, Stability
Sandalphon	Cherubim	Manifesting, Form

Table 3-1
Archangels and Order of Angels

Guide: *Archangel Khamael.* This wonderful assistant will keep you moving, activated and in alignment with the forceful energy that reminds you to release your inner-most self. When he appears he comes forward with fiery energy and in the form of a lizard, dragon or snake. He destroys imperfections and works with resistant energy to bring about a change. He will put you to the test for expansion of your True Will by agitating you until you see the path of your greater good. He is the ruler of Mars and the human beings, such as yourself, that are aligned with a need to move speedily through changes in order to purify and align with their soul pattern. Khamael oversees the consciousness of the Universe called Geburah (severity). Shiva is seen in the same conscious alignment as Khamael.

Challenge: When not utilizing your guardian for direction you may find yourself struggling with insecurities, frustrated with your world falling apart, involved in too many imperfections and entrapped with negative, mental dialogue. Fights, arguments, and self-destructive activities will be your focusing energy. You will wonder if there really is a God that can assist your pathway through this life-time.

Way Out: Align yourself with Khamael. Understand that your soul has chosen this pattern because it knows the path of your True Will is strong, powerful, aggressive and can work with, and withstand the forces of life. Come into your true identity by understanding your power, your strength and your inner wisdom. Ask yourself, "Am I destroying things in my life out of ignorance and an inability to see the True Light? Or, am I to destroy that which is in the way of my highest and best? (i.e., negative thoughts, poor attitudes and habits)." Stand in the position of courage and know your truth—it is from there that you can act from your True Will and bring forth your true identity.

Figure 3-1
Diane McPherson's Spiritual Guardian

Your Guardian Connection

Now is your opportunity to become aware of the guardian that supports you as you walk through this world. Keep in mind that this angel is the being you asked to help you stay on your path and complete the goal of your life lesson. You asked this being to help you meet obstacles in your pathway with strength, courage, and the ability to learn from the experience. You requested that your angel be at your side day and night, through times that are joyous and times that are fearful. You also asked that your guardian prompt you with challenges when you find yourself being complacent and unable to move forward. Your guardian is your staff of life, your connection to the Divine Creator.

Meditation

Sit or lie down. Listen to soft celestial music. (If you do not have this type of music, simply relax). Allow yourself to breathe with a steady relaxed rhythm and let your whole body become quiet and comfortable. Feel the sensation of floating on the mist of a beautiful white cloud. Let your experience continue and sense yourself traveling upward towards the farthest reaches of the sky. While you travel, repeat in a song-like fashion:

Guardian of mine
Being Divine
Come to me

Guardian of mine
Being Divine
Let me see

The Spirit of you
Flowing through
Supporting me

Guardian of mine
Being Divine
Come to me

Sing this several times. Angels like songs. They know when you sing you are connected to your heart, your soul, and to your purpose. Then respectfully request that you may see the Angel that is here to support your throughout your life. Ask to be allowed to know the Angel who is supporting your life lesson. Then become very receptive and be empowered by the presence of your guardian. Let colors, light frequencies, feelings, sound and sight into your realm of consciousness. Become acquainted with your guardian.

When you are complete, give thanks and note that each and every day you will connect with this divine being, who in turn will connect you with the God/Goddess of all life. Know that each and every day your guardian will assist you with walking your path and maintaining the awareness of your life lesson.

CHAPTER 4

Mystical Name, Mystical Numbers

Jane = 6/5/11 (4)

Expresses as a spiritual being with a loving consciousness that looks into the face of reality with new ways to change her experiences, create balance and express her wisdom for justice out in the world. She connects to the spiritual voice of union, is mentally adaptable, physically poised, well balanced, and organized within her inner consciousness, as she sees the world before her.

Your name provides the coding to identify you on many levels. When your name is spoken people get a picture or a feeling of you. They *know* you by your name. When you were born your parents' may have looked through a book of babies' names just to find the right name for you. Katherine, for instance, means purity. My mother saw me as an expression of purity. When I chose my firstborn's name it was Christopher, meaning Christ-like. I wanted him to be a loving citizen of the world.

Choosing a name is very important, for each name releases a vibration, a feeling, and a meaning. Everyone's name holds a hidden interpretation. Searching for a deeper understanding of names requires one to go beyond the baby book. In fact, our spiritual ancestors revealed that a key to unlock the innermost secrets of a name is through mystical knowledge of numbers. It is through your name that you outwardly express the "who" of you. You chose your name to depict yourself through an energy alliance. The ancient ones revealed that names had a numerological, energetic significance. In reviewing your name a numerical equation depicting the energy of spirit, mind, body and soul can be revealed. Also the archetypal nature of your name is exposed by decoding the numerical equation.

Pythagoras, Hindu priests, Tibetan monks, and Hebrew rabbis all expressed the importance of numbers as offering secret passageways into the understanding of life. They indicated that the spiritual, mental, emotional and physical components of life could be seen in numbers. They taught that numbers and letters vibrate at particular frequencies, and that certain letters and numbers vibrate at the same frequency. The study of numbers reveals "the structure of the universe and the essence of a person or object..." (June G. Bletzer, Ph.D., 1987:435). The structure of anything is vibratory at the subatomic level. Each structure has its own oscillation which creates a frequency. Each frequency can be connected to a number and reveal a hidden meaning.

An ancient system of number and letter correspondences, was chosen to interpret names as a method of discovering soul magic. Table 4-1 provides numerical values of letters. This association is based on theories by Gregg Tiffen, (*General Numerological Aspects,* paper presented at KAIROS Institute, 1987).

1	2	3	4	5	6	7	8	9	10
A	S	L	M	E	B	H	G	U	C
J	Z	T	N	F	D	X	R	V	K
I				P				W	O
								Y	Q

Table 4-1
Numerical Values of Letters

In this numerical system, interpretations of frequencies are revealed through a single number (except for 10 and 11 which are considered to be master numbers). Therefore, any double numbers are added to obtain a single digit. For instance, 12 is seen as 3 (1 + 2 = 3). These numbers are then matched to letters that inherently oscillate at a similar frequency as the number. Each letter and number take on a specific meaning. For instance, in Tibetan numerology the number 1 relates to the letters A, J, and I. Some metaphysical interpretations include: origination, independence, active, initiative, self, and consciousness. Table 4-2 reveals simple intrinsic meanings of numbers. An in-depth understanding of numerology is presented in the book and software program entitled, *Archetypal Numerology*, by Tom Brockriede & Katherine Torres, Ph.D. (Forthcoming.)

Further exploration of numbers also allows an understanding of the Archetypes of human personality traits. These prototypes can be reviewed and correlated through the TAROT system. This system not only investigates Universal principles, but also an individual's life passage from birth through cycles and phases of growth. It aids in the understanding and balancing of the inner and outer reality in order to obtain clear conscious awareness and oneness with the Divine Creator. Twenty-two archetypes are inherent within the TAROT and "...a way to personal growth through understanding of ourselves and life," can be depicted (Rachel Pollack 1980:9). In keeping with the Tibetan numerical system of eleven numbers for associations, a basic archetypal review and Universal principles of life are seen in the first eleven cards, (Table 4-3). The information provided is but a minor representation of a vast field of knowledge that Archetypal Numerology can provide.

The outward expression of a person is seen through their name. The interpretation of this name can be found in the metaphysical understanding of numbers. The first name provides information about the most positive expression a person wants for him/herself. The last name provides the energy aligned with challenges and work (or karma) to be experienced. Through a method of using consonants and vowels and combining them with numbers an energetic significance can be related through an equation.

Number	Description
1	Beginning, original, intent, attention, independent, active, self-conscious, initiative, intellectual; egotistical, unstable, stubborn, lazy
2	Subconscious, wisdom, memory, duality, polarity, dexterous, apathetic, vacillating, indifferent shy, cold, servile
3	Creative conscious, understanding, playful, youthful, mother/child, musical; worrisome, critical, vain
4	World consciousness, organization, stabilization, mercy, order, law; unorganized, dictator, disarray
5	Changes, adaptation, growth, activity, reality consciousness; conflicts, struggle, losses, severity
6	Union, communication, harmony, health, beauty, family; disharmony, separation, illness, repulsive
7	Intellect, student, victory, will, boundaries, Spiritual Consciousness, mystical, analytical; critical, daydreamer, over analytical, missed opportunities
8	Manifest, success, self-aware, rhythm, Higher Self, Lower Self, splendor, leader, strong, fearless; controlling, abusive, lusty, head-strong, selfish
9	Completion, foundation, fulfillment, sensitive, humanitarian, Holistic (mind, body, and spirit), psychic, creative; depression, aimless, aloof, insensitive, unrealistic
10	Unified and moving, new levels, futuristic, recycling; repeating old patterns; stuck in the past, egocentric
11	Universal completion, karma, idealistic, spiritual; shiftless, unjust, imbalance, fanatical

Table 4-2
Numerical Correspondences

Number	Archetype	Principle
1	Magician	Masculine, Will
2	High Priestess	Feminine, Wisdom
3	Empress	Mother, Creative
4	Emperor	Father, Power
5	Hierophant	Spirituality, Religion
6	Lovers	Social, Union
7	Chariot	Hero, Victory
8	Strength	Natural, Self Dominion
9	Hermit	Teaching, Sage
10	Wheel of Fortune	Timing, Cycle
11	Justice	Judicial, Refined

Table 4-3
Archetypical Review of Numbers

The equation is developed for understanding the spiritual, mental, and physical aspects of an individual. Then, by combining all of these numbers, a fourth level reveals the soul essence of a person. For instance, using the Tibetan numerical chart in Table 4-1, we can find the equation for the name of Jonathan (Table 4-4).

```
 10   1   1
J O N A T H A N = 3/10/4 (8)
1   4   3 7   4
```

Table 4-4
Deciphering Vowels and Consonants

First the vowels are added to obtain a spiritual connection. In this name the vowels are 10+1+1 which equals 12. Twelve is further reduced to a single digit, revealing 3 as the spiritual number. The consonants are then added to give the mental alignment. Here we find 1+4+3+7+4 equals 19 which is reduced to 10. Then the spiritual number and the mental number are added to obtain the physical number (3+10 = 13 reduced to 4). Adding them all we find 3+10+4 = 8 (reduced from 17), the soul number. Finally, it can be written as an equation: 3/10/4 (8). These numbers are further evaluated through word associations such as those in Table 4-2. Archetypal correlations are made by connecting the number to a Tarot symbol. For instance, the number 3 is associated with the Empress, 10 is associated with the Wheel of Fortune, 4 is connected to the Emperor, and 8 is the energy of Strength. Using Jonathan's example we could say that he is spiritually creative and nurturing. Mentally he is expansive and future-oriented. Physically he is grounded, organized, and an authority within his environment. From his soul level he is strong, intends to achieve self dominion, be creative, loving and natural.

Diane's Numerical Equation

As we continue to follow the pathway of Diane we can see how her name also supports her Life Lesson. The number 7 is connected to the Path of the True Will while 8 reminds her to take self-dominion as she grows in self-understanding. Such understanding will indeed help her respond to her soul level (the number in brackets) which again asks her to follow the path of the True Will. (Figure 4-1.).

Astrological comparisons are seen in Diane's numerical evaluation also. The Chariot corresponds to the element of Cancer, a co-ascendant for Diane. (Builders of the Adytum, Ltd., 1970). The number 10 is associated with Jupiter which rules Sagittarius (her moon). The eight is very significant. It is associated to the fiery spirit energy called Kundalini in Sanskrit. The spirit energy raises consciousness as it moves through an individual and the ability to take dominion over oneself occurs. As Diane's spirit energy arises she connects with her Life Lesson. Also of note for this eight, the Kundalini energy is seen as a rising snake. As you will see in Chapter 5, snake is Diane's animal nature.

Following the pathway of Diane allows you to recognize the dynamic intelligence of the soul. It shows that the alignment with Universal frequencies occurs over and over and that those frequencies serve a purpose in assisting the growth and achievement of a life experience.

Identity: *Diane = 7/10/8 (7) (Chariot, Wheel of Fortune, Strength).* Through your name we see that you move forward with knowledge of the True Will, expand yourself by revealing your abilities, and come forward with forcefulness and strength from your Higher Self to manifest your passion in the world of form. You are fast, sharp-witted, and able to take control of your environment. You are, indeed, a leader. You have abilities that can be seen as highly intuitive, mentally strong, and humanly successful.

Challenge: *McPherson = 6/4/10 (2) (Lovers, Emperor, Wheel of Fortune, High Priestess).* You can fall into aggravation through separation with your Higher Self. This separation keeps you from creating clear and focused thinking that allows you to expand your world and manifest successful endeavors. You will find yourself floundering, aggravated by a one-step-forward, two-steps-backward reality when you are in the negative of your identity. You will not know who you are, what your true will is, nor how to identify it. You will fight and struggle with your ego, your logical thinking and your ability to join forces with others to assist you in obtaining your highest and best. With the four and the ten in the negative, you will find it difficult to manage your business, money, and the affairs of security when you are in the negative of your identity. You will become scattered, flustered and stuck in the outer realms of thinking. You will dream of "what can/could be" and not get your innermost dreams grounded. You will speak and act from grandiose ideas. However, you will not utilize the tools that can provide you with the luxury and abundance that is available. You will not remember what is the proper guidance and connection to the True Will. You will not trust your intuition to lead you, balance you, and assist you in making clear and concise decisions.

Figure 4-1
Numerical Evaluation of Diane McPherson's Name

Way Out: Align with your energy of determination and connection with the wisdom of your True Self. Stick with your growth processes so you may expand and move into your true talents and true identity. Become self-aware and joyful in your ability to be in a state of self-dominion. Let the fire of passion and the expression of your true self move into the manifested reality of joy, power, strength, and force. Be who you truly dream of being. Set your boundaries to maintain a clear and focused direction of continuous movement, expansion, and manifestation of your inner most passions. Have fun. Enjoy the bounty that is yours.

Figure 4-1
Numerical Evaluation of Diane McPherson's Name
(continued)

Your Numerical Evaluation

Take this opportunity to create an equation of your name. First, work with your given first name at birth. How is it relating to the Life Lesson that was revealed to you during your meditation at the completion of Chapter 2? Then create and decipher your name as you are normally called by everyone. (For instance, though my first name is Katherine, for many years I was called Kathy. I, therefore, do the equations for both names in order to understand the energetic influence.) The name you normally go by is the one that has built the frequency of energetic exchange with Universal energies. Your first name depicts the most positive aspects of energy that you will use to help you be identified by others and align you with your life lesson while living amongst others.

Once you have your first name equated, work with your last name. It is the energy that will present the greatest challenge to you as you work toward achieving your life lesson. Its blessing is in keeping you moving forward through the challenges rather than allowing you to become complacent. Note that last names are often changed (due to step parents, marriages, or simply the desire to change a name.) Each change to your last name is an indication of karmic adjustment or completion and a movement toward other energetic patterns that can assist your life lesson.

With your first and last name equated you can make general assumptions as to the meaning of each number as it associates with your spiritual nature, mental acuity, physical and worldly endeavors, and the creative purpose of your soul.

How are you faring as you look at yourself?

Realizing that visible bodies are only symbols of invisible forces, the ancients worshipped the divine power through the lower kingdoms of nature... The sages of old studied living things to a point of realization that God is most perfectly understood through a knowledge of his supreme handiwork—animate and inanimate nature. Every existing creature manifests some aspect of the intelligence or power of the eternal one...

The Secret Teachings of All Ages by Manly P. Hall (Los Angeles: Philosophical Research Society, 1977, p. LXXXV.)

CHAPTER 5

ANIMALISTIC NATURE

BEAR

The bear hibernates through the winter trusting that the Life Force is caring for it and will awaken it to a new day and new experience in the spring. Bear knows how to go within to hear the inner message of the higher self and to trust the impulses that will reveal the direction to be taken. The Bear reveals an ability to be curious, cheerful, good-natured, fair, strong, and courageous. Native American lore states the bear was the head of the animal council and brought about great teaching and healing abilities.

Instinctual Self

Sometimes you just feel like an animal, don't you? You want to roar like a lion or be as quiet as a mouse. You could not survive the Earth realm without an instinctual nature. For this nature provides you with your ability to protect yourself, "fight or flee." Your survival needs are strong and when not fulfilled you are in fear. Instinctively you know when to dodge a falling rock, a swerving car, or remove yourself from the path of an on-rushing train. You suckled instinctively soon after your first breath to fill the needs of nourishment. You crawled, walked, and then ran; all with instinctive knowledge that these actions would get you somewhere.

When speaking of your friends and family you recognize particular personality traits of animals and use them to explain their actions, such as: "loyal as a dog", "independent as a cat," "courageous as a lion," "stubborn as a mule," "strong as an ox," "flighty as a bird" and so forth. These clichés speak an animal language.

The soul requires an instinctual nature when in the embodiment of a personality. This aspect allows it to survive the unknown experiences of the Earth. It also assists in a particular instinctual expression that will help a person exist within a specific personality trait such as the power and leadership of a lion, or the wisdom of a snake. By aligning with the frequencies of the Universe as a representation of an animal, the soul will choose what can best help its instinctual needs and assist its lessons in life.

As you enter the realm of Earth your consciousness aligns with other Universal and Earthly elements in order to understand and create form. The sacred power of the animal also provides a safe and powerful journey through a lifetime. Through the channeling process an animal is seen clairvoyantly. Its power is clairsentiently felt. Then through interpretations provided metaphysically, an understanding of the instinctual nature of the person is revealed.

Many cultures associate certain elements of the personality and personal power to animals. In Central American religious beliefs, "Every human being was thought to have one or more 'counterparts', mostly disguised as animals whose fates were linked to that of the human being in a manner conditioned by cosmic forces." (Ed. Geoffrey Parrinder, 1983:71) In the North American Indian tradition an animal vision depicts the power of a person. This power reveals a basic understanding of what they are to do or be in their lifetime.

As I trace the patterns of various individuals I find an animal nature always reveals itself. As the guardians of the Sacred Path Wheel indicate, the animal reveals the instinctive nature inherent in everyone. In the chart of Diane McPherson her animal nature reveals itself as a snake (Figure 5-1). In deciphering its correspondences I note that her instinctual nature is one of power, wisdom and the ability to change whatever is not working toward her highest and best in this incarnation. Her life lesson is to bring forth her inner identity. Certainly a way to bring that inner identity to her conscious reality is by eliminating what is not serving that purpose. Snake medicine reveals an inner nature as one connected with wisdom. In metaphysics the snake is understood to have the ability to know and understand the great mysteries of life. It represents an ability to change, be just, create healing, and to manifest Life Force Energy. Snake power creates healing on all levels, transmutes energy from the mundane to the beautiful, and brings about unmanifested realities into manifested form.

The snake is also connected to Diane's spiritual guide, Khamael. In *Angelology*, Khamael reveals himself in the form of a dragon or snake. The snake has long been associated with higher wisdom, the movement of spiritual energy from the base consciousness to higher consciousness. Interweaving of energy is thus seen between the snake and the guardian. Interweaving allows strength and endurance, lasting support, and a greater ability to take this journey. As we review her whole wheel we will see how the web of life was created to totally support her life lesson by the intelligence of her soul.

Everyone carries such instinctual intelligence. It is magical, and the mystical element of the animal nature is powerfully expressed in the way you survive.

Discovering the Animal in You

Instinctively you respond to life. It is your energy of protection, guidance and survival. As you connect with Earth, survival energy is necessary. The Earth is a life pattern of learning as you go. As you grow toward maturity, learning is without foresight. It is therefore necessary to take your steps forward with a power that can help you walk with an innate knowing of where you are to plant your next footprint on the path of life. So, what is your animal nature? What frequency of the instinctual vibrations of the Universe did you connect with?

Animal: *Snake.* Your instinctual nature is one of power, wisdom and the ability to change whatever is not working toward your highest and best in this incarnation. Snake medicine reveals your inner nature as one connected with true wisdom—the knowing of the True Will. With such an instinctual nature you are able to know and understand the great mysteries of life. Your instinctual self represents an ability to change, to be just, to create healing, and to manifest Life Force Energy. Within your natural self you can heal on all levels, transmute energy from the mundane to the beautiful, and bring unmanifested realities into manifested form.

Challenge: When misusing this power, you can cause a poison in situations, events, and people which can reach levels beyond repair. Care must be taken in knowing your true, instinctual nature. Responsibility is called for. When you are in the negative of your instinctual nature you will find yourself hiding, being ignorant, cunning, and radiating an emotionless force. You will strike with your poison by speaking before knowing, by being controlling or controlled, overpowering or powerless. You may butt your head against problems and force your way through them. However, you will never quite figure out what happened along the way. Such misuse of this force will keep you separated from your true spiritual nature and locked in the carnal/physical reality of strife and struggle of the Earth plane.

Way Out: Honor your instinctual nature. Get to know the power and wisdom that lies within. Call on the nature spirit of the snake to teach you of your unique medicine knowing. Become like the alchemist and transform your inner knowing to your outer reality. Manifest the True Life force within you in the outer world. Move with the power and the fire that snake represents. Be sensitive, flow with your psychic nature and transform. Be responsible with this great power. Don't let your ego get in the way. Release your True Will for it will produce the true power within.

Figure 5-1
Instinctual Nature of Diane McPherson

Journey Into Your Most Passionate Nature—Your Animal Self

Sit comfortably in an open armed chair. Let your breathing guide you into your own inner realms. Connect with the sacred place within you. Call on your Higher Self to reveal your instinctual nature. Ask that you see the true animal within you. As the animal nature is revealed to you, feel it rise inside you. Let your body become one with the animal. Are you a bird? Feel the flight. Are you a four-legged animal? Feel four legs walking. Allow yourself to shape shift into the animal of your instinctive nature. Allow yourself to dance the animal. Become it. Make sounds as it would make. If you are comfortable standing up through this session, then stand and dance your animal physically rather than within your mind.

Once you have connected with your instinctual nature you will enhance its power in your life. Maintain this power by being connected with your animal-self each day. Draw a picture of your animal in your journal. Make notes of everything you know about the animal of your instinctive nature. Research the qualities and habits of this animal and get to know yourself. Obtain a fetish of your animal and keep it near you to stir the memory and energy of support, power, passion and survival within you.

CHAPTER 6

HOW DOES YOUR GARDEN GROW?

Nature For Growth, Adaptation and Healing

What would it be like if you did not have the opportunity to grow? How frustrating to be trapped in a world of no growth, no advancement, no achievements. It would be very difficult to adapt to the environment around you. You would not understand hot or cold. You would not understand people and events. You would not know how to heal yourself physically, mentally, emotionally or spiritually. You would, indeed, be stuck.

It is the nature of living to grow, adapt, and balance through one experience after another in a lifetime. The plant world is the most recognizable display of this process. Plants, like humans and other aspects of nature express life as a cycle. They are seedlings in the womb of Earth, sprout into the birth of an individual plant (i.e., apple tree, carrot, bean, rose, or another plant), grow, are harvested, and die. Such a correlation can be seen in your humanness, as well. You are a seedling in the womb of your mother, you sprout through the birthing process, grow through childhood, adulthood, and the harvesting of your "ripe old age". You come to the end of your life and transit to another plane of existence through the process called death. The cycles of life are natural and are teachers of growth and adaptation.

As you enter the Earth plane you ask for assistance in growing and adapting to the world and environment in which you will live. That assistance comes through the Universal realm of Plant Energy. Your soul-knowing realizes the importance of growth. It realizes that through growth you will evolve to higher planes of awareness. Through adaptation your soul knows you will learn of your oneness with the many. Your soul also knows that through an Earthly existence the body will undergo adaptation and a need to stabilize and heal when the circumstances of change must re-establish the cellular system to higher vibrations. The experience of this change may bring about frustrations, confusion, illness and disease. Therefore, your soul connects with the spirit of the plant world to help your personality grow, adapt, and heal. This plant spirit will, in fact, be connected to the greater purpose of your life lesson.

In reviewing individual plants we can correlate and interpret one's ability to grow. For instance, a blueberry plant is well-rooted. It grows similar to a vine. It sprouts full leaves the first year and fruit within the second year before it dies back and hibernates until the next season. In looking to describe this nature as the growth and healing nature of a human being we could say that the personality is one who will grow and develop through an unfolding process. The person will grow best when in a cordial environment and intertwined with others (the blueberry vine grows around other plants very well). The person may show that they grow well when they have the opportunity to rest and recycle periodically. Because of the blueberry's medicinal properties as an astringent and tonic, we might see that the person needs to detoxify and revitalize periodically. Blueberry is also used to heal inflamed throats, intestinal discomforts, and body temperature imbalances. This may indicate problems that a person with a blueberry nature may inherently carry within their physical cellular system.

The Plant World of Universal Energy is the supporting energy for growth, adaptation, and healing as the soul travels through the realm of physical matter. Once again, through metaphysical understandings of plants an association can be derived in relation to the personality and life lesson. The plant also reveals a cosmic energy alignment that can be connected to the powerful forces of the planets and stars at the time of birth. For instance, the ivy plant is associated with the planet, Saturn. (Scott Cunningham, 1991:131.)

Reviewing Diane McPherson's chart in Figure 6-1, we can relate the powerful alignment the soul makes with the plant-spirit in order to assist growth, adaptation and healing. (Notice the closeness of the plant name to Diane's name as well as the zodiacal alignment. Spirit does work in mysterious and magical ways.)

Discovering Your Plant Essence

You are fully aware that you have come this far in your life by growing, adapting and changing whenever necessary to support your needs. Throughout this life experience you have found yourself in need of healing your body, circumstances, and events that seem to have rocked your essence of stability. Your soul chose a particular plant frequency of the Universe before you entered this Earth realm to help you. Throughout your life you have been using this element whether you knew it or not.

Not long ago while discussing a Sacred Path Wheel I had done for a woman she became very excited about the Mulberry plant being revealed as her supporting energy. She told me she loved the plant and had a mulberry tree growing right outside her meditation room. I was delighted to hear her story. For, indeed, as with her, your plant essence may be nearby and always ready to support.

Through meditation allow yourself to discover your plant world. Prepare your place of contemplation. Bring your journal to the event.

Center and align with your inner beingness. Breathe evenly in and out, and relax. Take a moment to be connected with your Higher Self. Imagine a great garden, bigger and more colorful than you have ever seen. It has trees, bushes, flowers, herbs, cactus, every imaginable plant. Walk through this garden and feel yourself connecting with these plants. One particular plant may stand out to you, call you to it, or in some way let you know it is connected with you. Go to this plant. Sit beside it and blend your energy with it. Feel how you balance with it. Ask it to give you its name. Ask your Soul-self to tell you why you chose it to assist you in this lifetime. Learn as much about it as you can.

When you feel as though you have completed your communication, leave the garden with gratitude and love. Allow yourself to return to the world of your conscious state. Let your breath be your guide to awareness.

Throughout the next several days research the plant that you have discovered. Investigate its traits both as a metaphysical and physical healer. If possible, discover its planetary connection and see if it aligns with your own astrological plan at birth. Fill your journal with the information and a drawing of your plant. Where possible, put this plant in your garden and let it radiate to you and blend with your own electromagnetic field. This will stimulate your soul alignment for growth and adaptation.

Plant: *Damiana.* This is a plant of great power. It carries a caution when utilized as a remedy for it can be overpowering, over stimulating, and should be administered with care. According to a Native American book on herbs, "Damiana often stimulates beyond the limit of our safe and healthy resources and encouragement beyond our natural energy level may have ill effects on the heart." (Alma R. Hutches, 1986:108). Through this you can see that your ability to grow and adapt is strong, forceful, and powerful. You can be easily aroused to move, to change, to adapt and to grow in any situation. You come forward with passion, joy, and youthful energy when you are on a growing campaign. Damiana healing powers are seen as a stimulant, tonic, aphrodisiac, a laxative, and as an assistant to migraines (an ailment of Aries personalities).

Challenge: When in the negative flow of your growth and adaptation, you will find yourself overwhelmed and over-powered. You may begin to withdraw and hold back. You will find yourself moving into fantasies and unfulfilled dreams. Your sense of worthiness will fall short. You will feel as though you cannot get to your true self and your true passion. This passionate self will be hidden beneath inappropriate sexual energy or the belief that you are inappropriately sensual/sexual. You will become rundown and impotent; you will start stuffing your emotions, and moving into the dream world and out of reality.

Way Out: Utilize this plant in your garden to revitalize soul memory. Call on the nature spirits of this plant world. Realign with your potent, natural self. Allow yourself to move through changes with exuberance, joy and passion. Bring your True Self out into the world—don't hide the real, passionate, and powerful you.

Figure 6-1
Diane McPherson's Supporting Plant

CHAPTER 7

YOU ARE A GEM

Similar to the plant and animal interpretations, gems can be likened to the human personality. In this relationship we find the mineral to be an identifying energy for strength and a foundation throughout the Earth experiences. Through the properties of a particular mineral, other identifying aspects of the individual are recognized. For instance, a rose quartz is defined as a healer of the heart. It opens the pathway for unconditional love. Its radiance brings about an ability to love oneself and share love with others. It can heal traumatized love relationships that stem from abuses experienced in childhood. It can attract interpersonal love relationships which each of us seek in order to balance ourselves.

Stones can be seen as a reflective power to assist further growth. Often times the stone associated with a person continues providing healing qualities similar to the plant world. One of my clients soul process was to bring the Jasmine plant to her energy field for growth and adaptation. This plant is known to assist balance and harmony for mind and body. In healing practices it is used to attune the balance for lungs, breasts, kidneys and problems of the nose and throat. From the mineral world she brought Blue Lace Agate. It, too, was revealed as a balancing stone and creates harmony in the mental, emotional, physical and spiritual bodies.

Other similar qualities of the stone and plant world relate to associations with the zodiac. One client revealed the plant world to be the Passion Flower for her growth and adaptive nature. Passion flower is ruled by Venus. Venus is a ruler of Libra. Her stone essence was the Diamond. It is considered one of the correspondences of Libra as well. Both were providing her the essence of growth and adaptation through connection with her Higher Self and reflecting Truth, Love, and clarity.

Early civilizations used gems regularly for healing or revealing the power of a person. Kings and Emperors used gems on their shields, staffs, crowns, and war gear. These gems would signify their status or the protection that they required to maintain their status. Thus, they saw the gems as a power tool.

Healing with stones has also been a long-time practice. Used in the early civilization of Atlantis and Lemuria, in Greek healing temples, and other cultures, stones provided just the right assistance for various diseases of the mind, emotions, body, or spirit. Quartz is known to have been used both in Atlantis and Lemuria. Clear quartz assisted the mind by clearing negative thought vibrations. Since it amplifies thought forms, it was used to transmit thoughts as well, assisting telepathic messages to safely connect with the person with whom one would want to communicate.

In ancient societies as well as our present time, stones have been used to heal a myriad of diseases. Heart ailments, for instance may require the connection with rose quartz or ruby. Both of these minerals carry the properties of opening the heart chakra and regenerating the tissue as they heal on a cellular level. Opening of the heart will certainly provide the individual with a greater capacity to love themselves and to love others. Also, an individual whose soul may request this stone for assisting a life lesson may also reveal the power of leadership with compassion and clarity.

Foundation of Strength and Personal Power

Stones are solid, dense, elements of the world. They reveal a particular quality of strength and power an individual carries. It is the energy the soul aligns with to create a strong foundation, that helps build the substance of the body and the world in which the individual will live. Stones are the concrete mass that solidifies the elemental potency of primitive Cosmic energies. As the stones harness these forces it is easier for the personality to use them. Through listening to stone energy a person will understand the intense force and even ancient life-stories that flow through the oldest element of Earth. Stones reveal the foundational energy one chooses to maintain balance and stability while traversing the physical realm. By correlating metaphysical interpretations of stones, one can find a connection to personality traits, and of course, to the life lesson.

As the stone world aligns with each person it presents a power essence. It reveals a particular quality of one's strength, magnifies it and reveals it to the world. The stone world provides the essence of one's foundation as s/he enters the realm of form.

As we return to view Diane's wheel of knowledge (Figure 7-1), we see that her choice for a foundational energy helps her maintain her strength and fortitude. It, in fact, helps her in being one with the True Will. Her soul-knowing certainly brought an alignment of great strength and purpose as it chose to blend with the mineral realm of copper. This great mineral is given the honor of carrying and connecting the energies of the masculine and ferninine forces of the Universe and forming a true channel of the Divine Will.

Stone: *Copper.* Copper can open the pathways to the True Will. It does this by connecting the masculine and feminine energies (Father Sky and Mother Earth). It is aligned with your moon sign, Sagittarius. Copper reveals your strength as a powerful, balancing and magnetic field of energy. Its healing qualities include releasing pent-up anger and unused power. It strengthens the body/mind. It is a healing agent for arthritis, stiffening joints, blood cleansing, and metabolism stabilization. It is considered an energy source for increasing your ability to know your True Will by knowing your feelings and releasing self-confidence. It also assists your ability to know your True Will by connecting you to the feminine/masculine energies within yourself.

Challenge: When not in alignment with your strength and copper-like abilities, you will find yourself out-of-sorts, angry, and unable to speak your truth. You will be inflexible, disconnected from your True Will, and either too logical or too irrational. You will not allow yourself to be in the channel of hearing, knowing, and being. You will not attract to you that which you need to manifest your heart's desire. You may find yourself having physical difficulties with stiffening joints, arthritis, metabolic disorders, and possible toxins running through your cellular system.

Way Out: Wear copper. Keep it in your line-of-sight. Call on the nature spirits of this mineral to direct you on the course of your personal power. Connect with True Spirit and you will connect with the True Will. Allow your masculine and feminine natures to merge and bring about the greatest power you can achieve. Be flexible, stable, and balanced in personal understanding.

Figure 7-1
Stone World of Diane McPherson

Finding Your Strength and Foundation

The stone world also holds great stories for you if you will allow yourself to listen to the stone people through meditation or by reading the markings on a stone. If you are a stone collector, gather all the stones and minerals of silver and gold that you have. Put them on a cloth before you. If you are not a collector, no matter. Simply allow yourself to mentally connect with the stones of the world. Ocean stones, Earth stones, gemstones, minerals of all kinds. Then feel yourself become centered in the midst of the stones as you move deeply within a state of meditation.

Imagine you are communicating with each and every stone and mineral you can see with your inner eye and feel with your inner senses. Let this world of stones and minerals communicate back to you. Let them send sensations and vibrational energies through you. Ask them, "Who amongst you did my soul align with to provide me strength, power and a foundation for living?" Silently and receptively await their answer.

Once you have connected to the stone energy of your soul-choosing, blend with it for a while. Feel the power that surges through you. Know its strength, for it is your strength. Connect with its energy that provides you with a foundation and stability for your continued growth and personal expression in the world. Get to know yourself through this stone.

When you feel complete in your communication, thank the world of stone people, thank your own soul-knowing, and thank the Spirit of All Life that has presented to each soul the multi-pathways of support. Then, return to your everyday awareness.

Write your messages in your journal. If you do not have the stone or mineral that was revealed to you, then obtain one. Keep it in your pocket or on your desk. Keep it where you can see it and connect it to the energy of your soul-knowing. This will rekindle the energy from within and help you reestablish your strength, your powerful foundational energy that you chose from the level of your soul intelligence before birth.

CHAPTER 8

FINDING A CONDUIT

A Channel For Entrance Into The Physical Realm

Preparation for embodiment includes finding a channel in which to focus energy for manifestation. Your soul has every intention of manifesting and bringing with it assisting energies to support its journey. It also carefully selects a conduit or conduits to center and focus the energy into the world of matter. The conduits are associated with six directions: north and south, east and west, above and below. One or more of these portals are used to channel the energies for your travels through the Earth existence.

In Native American or Celtic lore four to seven directions of energy fields are used to obtain balance and connection with all life. These directions are *north, south, east, west, above, below,* and *within.* They represent a psychological and spiritual understanding of the process of life. By following the path of a circle from east to north and connecting to the center we can associate the following:

East. This direction represents the rising of a new day, the beginning of a new experience or a new birth. It represents illumination and mind expansion. From an elemental standpoint it is air and supports the mental aspects of humanity. It is also connected to the season of spring.

South. This direction represents growth and adaptation in the world in which one lives. It is the child developing into an adult. South represents the energy that one uses for motivation. With it one can connect and interact with others along the path. South teaches trust. As one moves and develops, south provides opportunities to fulfill one's desires. The elemental aspect of the south is fire, the spirit within that moves and provides inspiration to keep on growing, adjusting and understanding life. This quadrant represents the summer season.

West. This direction represents the adult level of ourselves and the opportunity to reap the rewards for one's work and achievements as a person develops through life. It is the time when a person receives recognition and offers knowledge to others so that they may learn as well. The elemental aspect of this direction is water and represents the emotional self as well as our creative and intuitive expressions. West is associated with the fall season.

North. This direction represents the elder aspects of humanity and the opportunity to retreat from the forces of achievement and strenuous work. It is the time one receives respect and, again, offers wisdom to those younger than themselves to help them walk the path of awareness. It is also considered the place of ending—death, in preparation for rebirth. Its elemental aspect is Earth, the place of rest, peace and quiet. It is the direction of wisdom—which comes after long journeys and experiences. Through Earth, it is also the association of the body and the world in which one lives. It reminds one to care for the body as the temple of life and to work with the nature spirits, humanity, and life as a whole. North is the season of winter.

Above. In every spiritual association with this direction the above energy connects humanity to the creator of life—God, the masculine energy of the Universe. It directs, inspires, focuses and channels energy.

Below. This direction is associated with Earth Mother, the Divine Goddess energy that births, preserves and nurtures the life-force energy in all forms. Below represents the feminine energy in all life. It supports your receptive processes and teaches you how to love, adjust to changes, and support others as well as accept support in your life.

Within. Represents the energy within one's own space where the connection with the Higher Source of consciousness can be made. It is within that you hear the inner voice of higher guidance and allow yourself to respond more clearly to life.

The directions from soul intelligence reveal a channel or channels in which the soul pilots Universal energies. They are the conduit(s) for Divine Energy to transform itself from formlessness into form. These energies are used to align with form and the materialization of the physical body. Also, these directions assist the personality and support life experiences, providing direction and power for Earthly stabilization.

At the time of entrance into the Earth realm the soul follows a particular direction (or directions) of energy. The direction(s) serves the individual throughout a life-time as additional energy of power and protection. Each time an individual connects to the directions of soul-choice they feel the empowerment. Through the review of metaphysical correlations of energies, associations are made and interpretations are formed for further understanding the soul purpose.

Diane's directional alignment was with one portal only. Through her soul choice a powerfully directed energy was chosen. As has been noted, South is a portal for the energy of Fire. This is a correlation to her astrological sign, Aries, her animal, and her Spiritual Guardian. Here we note how the soul interweaves powerful alignments to assure the completion of the goal for the soul.

Direction: *South.* This is a direction of fire, movement, growth, and adaptation. It is a very creative energy pattern because it utilizes the inner nature of the child-self. When bathed in this energy you bring the path of the True Will into the world of form. It is the place of strength, power, sensitivity, and generosity. This energy teaches you about the physical realities in which you live. It provides you with discipline, full attention, and determination to reach your goals. It helps you align with the path of your True Will by bringing about clear sight and determination through lessons learned.
Challenge: When not aligned with your sacred energy of the south, you will experience traumas, abuses, emotional and physical harm, anger, frustration and undisciplined reactions to life. You will not want to learn or will attempt to learn too quickly without concentrated effort. You will hold in your feelings or yell them out and hurt others with your fiery tongue. You will be blunt and unthinking in your exchange with other people, or locked into fear that what you say holds a string of retaliation. Physically you will find it difficult to maintain a healthy, vital, and strong body. Mentally, you will have difficulty staying with the program of a clearly focused mind, and spiritually you will feel disconnected from your Higher Self and the direction and identification of your True Will.
Way Out: Connect daily with the energy of the south. Feel the flow of the energy through your body. Be in alignment with your youthful, exuberant self. Allow yourself to learn, adapt and grow in any given situation without guilt, undue criticism, and fears. Express yourself openly. Be clear thinking and release your emotional capacities for love, loyalty, generosity and kindness. All of this will help you align with your inner identity and know your True Will. (Note: Snakes are a part of the south energy alignment in the Native American spiritual understanding of the wheel of life.)

Figure 8-1
Directional Energy of Diane McPherson

Experiencing Your Conduit

Bring to your meditation space your journal and pen. Also, if you have acquired your plant, stone, and a replica of your animal nature, I would suggest you bring them also. Set them on a cloth before you in the middle of the room where you meditate.

Today I ask you to think about your room as a circular energy. Note where the east, south, west, and north quadrants are, once again. Place yourself in the center near your objects. Stand and face the east. Connect with the east and ask of the Universe to open the portal of the east energy that you may feel its flow. Then turn to the south and do the same. Continue through the west and the north. Then stand in awareness of the direction above you and below you and once again ask the Universe to open these portals. Feel the energy of your inner sanctuary and state that this portal of inner awareness is open to you as well. (Katherine Torres, Msc.D., Ph.D., 1994, 3-10.)

Sit down in the center of this circle and feel the energy flowing from all directions. One or more of six directions were chosen by your soul as the conduit for the Universe to use. This conduit provided the channel of all energies your soul would use to vivify its purpose for incarnation. The energies of your guardian, your name, instincts, and so forth came through these portals.

While meditating and feeling these energies, ask of your soul-knowing which one or more portals were chosen as your entrance channel(s). You will recognize the portal(s) because a dynamic flow of energy will occur from the direction(s) of choice. Allow yourself to become one with the energy.

When you feel complete in your knowing give thanks to the Divine for this revelation. Know that in this moment you have gathered strength and power to step forward in your day as the True You. Return to your daily conscious state with this strength and knowing.

Each and every day before you enter the world of activity, connect with your portal(s) of energy. Let this energy flow through you. Let it vitalize you and empower you for the activities ahead.

My own directional energies are above, below, and east. As I begin my day I routinely connect with these directions. I feel the energy from above flow through me. I then ask for the energy below to flow upwards and connect with the above field. Then I connect with the east and feel the east winds flow around me. After these energy patterns combine I visualize my animal standing beside me. I am energized and strengthened as I prepare to meet the daily activities ahead of me.

CHAPTER 9

SACRED SYMBOL

Findings during channeling reveals that each person possesses a symbol within their cellular system. The symbol is composed of a triangle, a circle, or a square and can be seen in one or all three geometric shapes. For instance, one person may simply release the symbol of a triangle from their cellular center. Yet, another person may release a circle within a square. Some individuals may reveal combinations of the three. Each symbol contains an alignment with cosmic laws.

Sacred Law

A triangle represents Sacred Law. Sacred Law is the true nature of the Universe. It encompasses all forms of existence, is non-judgmental, constant, perfect and unchangeable. It is the Law of Laws—the Law of Love. It holds all life sacred. It is the highest form of spiritual alignment that is known to humanity.

Natural Law

A circle represents Natural Law. This law depicts the continuous expansion and contraction of Universal energy. Its constant fluctuation governs involution and evolution, humanity's perception of time and space, cycles and phases, death and birth, and all awareness of life. It is revealed in the Law of Cause and Effect. This Law states that for every action there is an equal reaction. We simplify it by saying whatever goes out comes back. Within this law is the energy of karmic experiences, reincarnation, and evolution of consciousness.

Human Law

A square represents Human Law. Human Law determines the form and density of bodies and the social structure that governs humanity. It is the only law that is influenced by human concepts of order and logic. It is changeable and transient. It asks that the individual abide by the laws of the land. It regulates all systems within humanity. Systems that govern our life such as school systems, county regulations, systems that regulate the processes of computers, any system that one can think of falls under Human Law. Also, under Human Law, humanity is charged with the care of the Earth, the assisting of the growth of animals, and plants, the care taking of the stone world, and the sharing of life with other human beings. As caretakers this law asks that humanity learn how to recycle, regulate use of ozone killers, monitor our willingness or selfishness to know we are a part of the whole and the Earth must be taken care of in order for the soul to live in a wholistic environment. By honoring Human Law one becomes aware of the axiom, "that which is above is that which is below."

A symbol or combination of symbols reveals the law or laws that a person is to learn about, abide by and honor throughout his/her incarnation. It, too, can be correlated to the life lesson.

Entering into the realm of physical reality you come forward under the alignment of Sacred Law, Natural Law, or Human Law. The journey into the physical realm requires you to associate, abide by, give particular importance to, and understand a law or laws in this lifetime. In fact, following the laws with conscious intent will allow positive alignment with your life lesson. When a particular symbol is missing from the cellular level of a person it may reveal that they have already learned that law and will not depart from it in this life time. It may mean that it simply is not time to learn this law yet. It may even mean that the Universe is taking care of that law for you.

As we look at Diane's chart we recognize that she works with Sacred Law and Natural Law (Figure 9-1). It is truly by focusing on these laws that she will understand True Will and be connected to the powerful direction of Pure Spirit.

Your Sacred Symbol

Be sure to bring your journal for this meditation. I would also encourage you to bring colored pencils. When you connect with your sacred symbol draw it in your journal and color it.

Prepare yourself to enter your sacred place of meditation. Let your breath be the guiding energy to the still, quiet place within. When you have reached the place of your inner sanctuary, allow yourself to watch for your symbol. Feel and visualize yourself searching through your cellular system. Ask for the guidance of your Higher Self to lead you to the cell that will reveal your sacred symbol. Flow through the vision and experience. When you become aware of your symbol blend with it. Feel it. Trace its lines with your inner feelings. Awaken to the sense of the Law or Laws that you chose to align with in this life. Are you consciously living them? Make a commitment to daily be aware of how you are supporting these laws in your activities, associations, and personal connection to the Universe.

Return to ordinary consciousness and draw your symbol in your journal. Take the time to become creative with it. Become familiar with the law or laws associated with your symbol. Consciously act upon these laws in your daily activity.

Symbol: *Circle within a triangle.* You are here to work with, learn from, and master Sacred Law and Natural Law. Sacred Law is the Law of Laws. You master it through love and by honoring all life. Symbolized by the triangle, Sacred Law encompasses all forms of existence, is non-judgmental, constant, perfect and unchangeable. Natural Law is depicted by the circle and reveals the continuous expansion and contraction of energy. This constant fluctuation governs your perception of time, cycles, seasons, birth, transformation, and your awareness of all life. Natural Law governs intelligence and teaches you to learn the meaning of the mind, its functions both logically and creatively, and its ability to overcome struggle and frustration.
Challenge: When not aligning, learning, and following the boundaries of these laws, you will find yourself in constant struggle and traumatic experiences. You will not feel loved or loving. You will find yourself expressing selfishness and separation. You will be unmotivated and discouraged with the process of life. You will fall short or over extend yourself in many activities. You will feel as though you are just about to make it and then have a collapse to your adventure. Timing will become a problem for you and you will seem to miss opportunities by being just a few seconds ahead of or behind the event. Because of the contraction-expansion process of Natural Law, you will find that physically you have difficulty maintaining a balanced body weight, eat too little or too much, exercise too much or too little, etc. Mentally you will experience an over-abundance of thoughts such as a chattering mind, or a dulled, expressionless thought pattern. Emotionally, you will have too many highs or too many lows and depression may become a problem. Spiritually, the True Will will be an illusion and just out of your reach.

Figure 9-1
Diane McPherson's Sacred Symbol

Way Out: Align and work from Sacred Law and Natural Law. Come from a space of unconditional love and understanding of all life. Always work with your spiritual sources and find the sacredness in everyone and everything you encounter. Through Natural Law come to an understanding of the ebb and flow of all things. Work with your own biorhythm: learn to be active when you feel energetic and rest when your body requires relaxation. Understand and honor time and space and at the same time learn to move beyond them through the expansive nature of the Universe. Work with the nature world and the cycles and phases of all life. To enhance the stability of your body, eat the foods in season for they will be aligned with the cycles of Natural Law. Understand timing. Be on time and in time for all events the Universe offers you. Come to know abundance, for Natural Law can provide abundance. However, when in the negative of it, it can take it away as quickly as it presented it to you.

Figure 9-1
Diane McPherson's Sacred Symbol
(continued)

CHAPTER 10

KNOWING

Intuitive Power

Beyond basic instinct is the essence of *knowing* and a connection to the Higher Being within. This knowing is intuition. Each person has within themselves an intuitive nature that can be used to give direction for growth on a daily and life-time basis. Understanding the basic intuitive process also provides insight to inner energy patterns that assist the life lesson. June Bletzer describes intuition as, "a non-thought which by-passes the process of thinking and brings through a whole body sensation of 'this information is important'" (1987:323).

Your intuitive power is your alignment with True Spirit and reveals the way in which you can have insight to your path walk. It is your inner dialogue. Knowing your intuitive nature can assist you in living your sacred path more significantly. It can help you manifest your desires, and can help you stay in alignment with your True Self, and companions of choice (seen or unseen).

Each person works with their own unique powers of knowing. Diane's intuitive nature reveals her soul choice for knowing how to maintain connection with her Higher Power and the inner knowing of how to take each step upon her pathway. For Diane it is working with her well-developed logical mind and connecting it to her intuitive mind. Having known Diane for several years I am very impressed by her ability to use her logical mind and poetically express her knowledge. This oxymoron is a typical example of her intuitive nature.

Your intuitive nature: *Balanced logical and intuitive knowing.* Your intuitive power comes from a learned process of cognitive thinking connected with the surges of inner feeling/knowing. It is at its highest point when you connect with what you know and when you come from *cause* rather than effect. This will affect change in any event you are experiencing in your life at any given moment. Such a nature is centered, compassionate, loving, and whole.

Challenge: When disconnected from your intuitive nature you will find yourself frustrated and trying to "figure" things out from a logical or irrational base. You will become disconnected from people, circumstances or events going on around you. Your frustration will leave you isolated and separated from the sources that can truly help and give you guidance. This will cause you to be emotionless, closed, and out-of-balance on many levels. You will come from a low sense of esteem and integrity.

Way Out: Balance and blend your logical mind with your intuitive mind. Let your visioning be assisted by your planning. This will allow you to get to a place of centered knowing and powerful expression of your True Will. You will clearly understand your inner identity and express yourself from a position of strength, power, force and love.

Figure 10-1
Diane's Intuitive Process

Discovering Knowing

Everyone is connected to a sixth sense—a knowing deep within. We call it intuition and quite often give women credit for having it and forget that men have it too.

When connected with your *knowing* you may wonder what it means, you may not be able to explain it, however you do have a distinct sense that it is correct and directive. Responding to this knowing assists in magnifying your awareness of it. The more you use it, the stronger it gets. The more you declare it the less often you deny it.

Getting to know your intuitive nature is much easier than you realize. Intuitive processes can be narrowed down to three phases: clairsentient, clairvoyant, and clairaudient. When one has mastered these phases union with Higher Self occurs and a fourth step, the state of clairgnosis is quite easily experienced.

The clairsentient intuit feels knowledge. It flows through the whole body and provides an energetic response of "I know". Some people express this as a "gut" feeling or "heart" feeling. Others feel the energy surging or tickling from their feet to their head.

A clairsentient person is aware of the emotional state of other people, the energy within a room or group, and is well connected with the magnetic energy surging through the Earth. When remembering a person, circumstance or event a clairsentient will lower their eyes in a gesture of trying to feel the memory. Clairsentience is the most common intuit process and is truly felt by all people. I have found that people who are clairsentient tend to deny their intuition more than those who are clairvoyant or clairaudient. (Though it does seem that each person has their own state of denying their intuitive process.)

The clairvoyant intuit is visionary. They tend to see knowledge through symbols, inner visions, and insights. Often they are telepathic. When an incident is described to them, they will see the incident in their mind. When remembering events they will usually raise their eyes recalling through vision what they have done. Interestingly, a clairvoyant person knows that what they see intuitively is truly beyond their personal capabilities. They will, however, tend to believe that they are imagining or fantasizing what they see. It is their job to move beyond illusion by applying the knowledge that they receive to their world. If it works it is truth. If it does not work it is likely imagination and further training is required to specialize their gift.

The clairaudient intuit hears the knowledge from within. A voice speaking to them of an event prods them to respond to their intuition. At times they will feel as though they heard someone call their name, voice a particular direction to take in their life, or even hear a hum or buzzing sound in their ear before receiving insight to some event. When remembering a circumstance in their life, a clairaudient person will have a tendency to look side to side as if searching for a sound to direct their memory. In fact, their eyes tend to drift from ear-to-ear. For a clairaudient, they must train themselves to understand the inner guidance that comes from the Voice Within. Our society has created a supposition that anyone hearing voices may be insane. Though I would not discount the existence of psychotic experiences when a person is truly mentally ill, I would say that it is important to understand that a person who hears an inner voice may, in fact, be clairaudient and able to *hear* intuitive messages rather than sense or see.

Most people have a combination of these intuitive processes. One will be stronger than another. I, for instance, *feel,* which becomes a *vision,* and then I am able to hear thoughts or words and translate what I have just seen or felt. I do not always "hear". Most of the time I have to translate what I feel or see.

As the person develops and evolves to higher spiritual levels of consciousness the form of clairgnosis occurs. Clairgnosis is wholistic knowing. No words, sensations, or visions occur. Simply, an instant and profound knowing is present. There are no questions in this state—there are only answers. When one reaches clairgnosis, clairvoyance, clairsentience, and clairaudience simply dissolve and are left behind. Soul integration occurrs with clairgnosis. In its early stages a person may find they slip back and forth between clairvoyance and clairgnosis. However, as the integration solidifies mastery occurs and clairgnosis is stabilized.

How Do You Intuit?

Prepare your place of meditation. Sit comfortably and relax. Let go of all extraneous thoughts. Become aware of your breathing and allow it to flow in and out rhythmically. Let your breath quiet you and move you into your own inner sanctuary. Ask that you be connected to your Higher Self.

Once relaxed and centered recall yesterday evening. Remember what you were doing and how you were preparing for dinner. What did you eat? Where did you eat? Who was with you?

As you ponder this memory, sense your inner response. Do you feel, see, or hear? Are you trying to sense something from within your body? Are you visualizing the place, food, and people? Are you hearing the clanking of dishes, silverware or dialogue you had with someone else? Remain in a state of recall until you become aware of your stronger senses.

Allow yourself to be aware of your breathing, your room, and your ordinary sense of consciousness and return to the now.

After you have become aware of your own sensation through reflection, realize how you intuit. Were you clairsentient, clairvoyant, or clairaudient? Were you a combination? If you realized you were a combination, which came first?

Practice daily responding to your intuitive nature. Keep in mind that the more you respond the stronger your intuitive nature becomes. The stronger your intuitive nature becomes the greater your connection to your soul-knowing and your spiritual alignment.

CHAPTER 11

THE GATHERING OF PEOPLE

Interpersonal Relationships

Other people assist you throughout your lifetime and life lesson. The Earth realm is about "the many," not just one. People in your life are teachers and reflectors. They help you recognize yourself. They teach you about forming states of union. Companionship helps stir the desire to return to the One. To return to the God/Goddess All There Is, you must understand union. To understand union, you need to interrelate with others.

Understanding personal attributes for relating helps you express yourself more clearly and with personal power. Knowing what challenges you face in relationships helps you become aware, able to heal and more clearly align with your ability to communicate within any relationship.

How you relate to others—your significant other, siblings, children, peers, parents, and acquaintances—is revealed in the Sacred Path Wheel. It shows the reflection that others bring in teaching you who you are. Often this knowledge reveals the assistance others give in teaching you your life lesson. Interpersonal relationships provide the opportunity to heal karmic deeds. No person in your life is without a gift of knowledge to you and you to them. Every interaction, communication, and sharing provides a teaching, an opportunity for you to be recognized, and a way for you to see the reflection of your God-Self.

Review Diane's relationship process (Figure 11-1). Note how it connects to the information already gleaned. The statement, "Relate without defense," connects to the astrological elements of Aries and Mars, as well as the snake, and Khamael seen in her Sacred Path Wheel. She learns, as she contemplates her power in interpersonal relationships, that without defense tactics she is better able to connect to her true inner identity and to the True Will.

How Do You Relate?

Allow yourself to reflect on your present interpersonal relationships. Pay attention to your recollection of communication. When is communication open and flowing? When is it stifled and a struggle? Review the significant people in your life and how you interact with them.

As you review each person in your life, write about the strengths and weaknesses you see in each of them. List their communication skills, the way they balance their life, and their idiosyncrasies. List everything you can about the individuals who bring themselves into your life. Go over your notes and ask how many times you have repeated a strength or weakness. Look at the circumstances that brought these people into your life. What significant events flow from your memory. What happened throughout the event?

As you reflect you will begin to see a thread of consistency. A message of relating will occur. Write it down. Write down the positive aspects of that method of relating. Write down the challenges. Then ask yourself, "Has this interpersonal way of relating been a consistent method of communication with others in my life?" If it has, you have likely fallen upon your soul desire for relating to others in this lifetime. You have discovered the way that relating to others can help you achieve your life lesson.

Take a few moments to energetically and visually connect with these participants in your life. Send each of them a heart-felt thank you. Let them know you appreciate their supporting energy even when it is challenging. And let them know that you are glad that you are participating in their life and helping them achieve their goals as well.

Relationships: *Relate without defense.* Relationships provide you with the opportunities to get to know yourself through others. From the most positive nature of relationships you have the opportunity to express your true inner identity. You respond to the alignment of your True Will when you allow yourself to be patient, accepting, and utilize your ability to see the bigger picture as it relates to those with whom you spend time. Your strongest relating power comes when you let your defenses down and play in the network of relationships. Each opportunity, obstacle, and event in a relationship provides a new and wonderful unfoldment of yourself.
Challenge: An inability to communicate without being defensive and ready for an argument, or wanting to escape from interactions and be alone will be a challenge. When you feel unable to get to the bigger picture you will struggle with the learning process of others. You will not understand that knowledge is being provided to you by being connected to others. You will try too hard to make a relationship work, forcing it to move forward when it needs to be still. Or, you will find yourself unmoving and unwilling to end a relationship for fear that another will have dominion over you. (Indeed this action/nonaction will allow them to take dominion). Your willfulness will begin to flourish, self-centered thinking will bring about an inability to understand another, and the gateway to a new expression will seem locked.
Way Out: Release defensive, war-like tactics. Open yourself to new experiences—even if the road is not clear and the pathway not evident. Rise above your fears and you will see the reason for every interaction and how it assists you in knowing who you truly are. It allows you to take dominion through love, understanding, and open communication. You will then align with a comprehension of wills—your will, their will, and the True Will.

Figure 11-1
Diane's Interpersonal Relationship Directive

Review Diane's relationship process (Figure 11-1). Note how it connects to the information already gleaned. The statement, "Relate without defense," connects to the astrological elements of Aries and Mars, as well as the snake, and Khamael seen in her Sacred Path Wheel. She learns, as she contemplates her power in interpersonal relationships, that without defense tactics she is better able to connect to her true inner identity and to the True Will.

How Do You Relate?

Allow yourself to reflect on your present interpersonal relationships. Pay attention to your recollection of communication. When is communication open and flowing? When is it stifled and a struggle? Review the significant people in your life and how you interact with them.

As you review each person in your life, write about the strengths and weaknesses you see in each of them. List their communication skills, the way they balance their life, and their idiosyncrasies. List everything you can about the individuals who bring themselves into your life. Go over your notes and ask how many times you have repeated a strength or weakness. Look at the circumstances that brought these people into your life. What significant events flow from your memory. What happened throughout the event?

As you reflect you will begin to see a thread of consistency. A message of relating will occur. Write it down. Write down the positive aspects of that method of relating. Write down the challenges. Then ask yourself, "Has this interpersonal way of relating been a consistent method of communication with others in my life?" If it has, you have likely fallen upon your soul desire for relating to others in this lifetime. You have discovered the way that relating to others can help you achieve your life lesson.

Take a few moments to energetically and visually connect with these participants in your life. Send each of them a heart-felt thank you. Let them know you appreciate their supporting energy even when it is challenging. And let them know that you are glad that you are participating in their life and helping them achieve their goals as well.

CHAPTER 12

STATE OF UNSELFISHNESS

Gift to Humanity

As a you evolve you move beyond the focus of yourself and into the service of others. Every human being has a gift to give humanity. Your gift-giving process helps others as well as it helps you. It, of course, supports your life lesson and assists your soul growth.

Although not necessary, your gift to humanity can be found in your career. It may also be seen by volunteer work, or perhaps simply during the course of a conversation. A gift certainly will be given by the example you demonstrate through living your truth. Each time you "walk your talk" you are providing a message of confidence and encouragement to others to do the same. That, in itself, is a wonderful gift.

Throughout the research of Sacred Path Wheels the gift to humanity is seen as the outward expression of a person's life lesson. Particularly as a person enhances their own growth by living the positive potential of their life lesson, their gift becomes more focused.

Most individuals believe that their gift to humanity is their purpose for being on the Earth. *Au contraire*. Their gift is the reward for following their life lesson. The life lesson is very self centered. It is geared toward the individual soul growth for the return to the One Great Creator. The Gift to Humanity is the door to the Union with the One

Great Creator. Once a soul has recognized its purpose (life lesson) and realized the importance of the return to Oneness, s/he will know that there is importance in serving others. The importance is the knowing that WE ARE ALL ONE, and until we are all ready to move to the higher space of Union, each individual soul must help. This help is a loving gift. Through this act of gift-giving the doorways open to the Union with the TRUE SELF.

When the gift to humanity is known, it can be honored. Such honoring of the gift becomes like a fine diamond, giving light to those who have eyes to see and a heart to receive. As each person opens their own self to gifting without thought of something in return, an unconditional love arrangement occurs. This energy flowing back and forth between individuals allows the collective unconscious to raise its vibration and thus help all souls grow, evolve and recognize the Path of Return to the One Great Spirit.

Diane McPherson's gift to humanity, Figure 12-1, is truly heightened by her knowledge of her Life Lesson—to bring forth her inner identity. Through knowledge of her True Self she is able to recognize a uniqueness. This uniqueness she is also able to see in others and reveals it to them and to other people. Such sharing by Diane announces talents of the individuals she knows and opens others to recognizing their talents, as well.

Here again I am privileged to know Diane. She, in fact, does share and encourages the unique talents of others. She gifts her gift often and it is pleasant, rewarding, and even educational. As she gathers with others she shares knowledge from other teachers, she tells of talents of individuals she is acquainted with, and if she finds a particular author's information to be transformative, she is sure to tell her group of friends and acquaintances. Her enthusiasm is catching and others are rewarded by her sharing.

What Is Your Gift?

Whether you realize it or not you are gifting to humanity all the time. Deep within you have a compassion for others and a desire to help them have the best experiences life has to offer. Just as you want happiness for yourself, you want happiness for others. Your compassion is a gift.

Also, you have a very special gift, unique only to you. It is the pattern your soul chose as part of the webbing of your wheel of life. You may be a healer, a writer, a teacher, a counselor. You may be a chef, a scientist, a gardener, or a steadfast reflection of poise and confidence for others to use as a guiding post. Whatever it may be, knowing it will increase your opportunity to gift more often.

Take the time to write the many ideas you have about how you gift to humanity. In what ways do you serve others? In gifting to others, what gives you the most joy and love swelling within your heart? Is there one central theme that strikes you? Does it seem to tie in with the Life Lesson you have discovered?

Now is the time to take an inner journey to reflect on your Gift to Humanity.

Prepare your sacred space and time for meditation. Relax. Become totally comfortable and feel yourself moving your consciousness inward to your inner silent place.

In this quiet place ask your soul-self to step forward. Invite your soul-self to take you on a journey to review your gift to humanity. Then sit back and allow the journey to unfold for you. Don't question, worry or direct it. Simply allow 10 to 15 minutes to elapse for the experience. Allow your soul-self to impress you with thoughts, feelings, and pictures.

When your time has completed for the journey, give thanks for knowledge gained and return to your ordinary conscious state. Write down what you have received. Review how often in your life you have acted out your gifting. Then take it to heart and perform your act of gifting frequently and with conscious knowing. Always gift with unconditional love. The rewards will be great.

Gift: *Create innovative support systems to reveal the talents of others.* Express to people their uniqueness. Honor their talents and show them ways to be productive with their special gifts. Utilize the talents of your own powerful, logical and expressive mind to provide ideas and ways and means for people to perceive the way in which they can express their abilities.
Challenge: When you are not gifting to humanity you will find their talents envious. You will feel yourself shying away from others with gifts to share and find them untrustworthy. You will be skeptical of others. You will not be supportive of others and your own unique self will become hidden as well.
Way Out: Express the uniqueness of others to them. Honor their special talents by being supportive. Reveal to them ways and means for sharing their abilities with the world. Creatively become involved with others and their abilities. You may even want to become an agent for others talents.

Figure 12-1
Diane's Gift to Humanity

CHAPTER 13

UNIVERSAL LIGHTS

Manifesting, Healing and Expressing Your Personal Power

You are a light unto the world. Your electromagnetic field emits a kaleidoscope of colors. These colors are enhancing energy as you live each day in a world of unknowns. The colors that emit from you illustrate strength, purpose, healing and manifesting support. Though your electromagnetic field has several striations and colors, three important levels and colors are explored in the Sacred Path Wheel. They are the colors that your soul chose to enhance your ability to co-create and manifest, to heal mental, emotional, and physical imbalances, as well as to express your personal power out to the world.

Light frequencies surround everyone and everything. "Color is a strong subtle force shaping human behavior;" (Bletzer 1987:122). Connecting to color stimulates various responses from within you that can assist in changes, activation of desires, and healing. Light is the higher power that surrounds all of us and emits in colors.

In the research of the Sacred Path Wheel it was discovered that the spectrum energy from the Universe provides assistance to the soul journey as well. The light of the Great Spirit is a brilliant white. As it expresses itself through the spectrum of colors it gives aid to certain levels of existence. The soul, in its ever-intelligent alignment with the Great Spirit, and for the purpose of entering an Earthly pathway, aligns with color essences. These colors, when used through decorations, clothing, lighting, and meditation enhance personal energy. The colors also stir soul-memory and stimulate connection with the Higher Self of an individual.

Each color frequency provides characteristic patterns. In the following table a rainbow of colors are given and some correlations for understanding how they affect life experiences. This is just a minor discussion on colors. There are many points of view as to the meaning of colors and those interested in knowing more would be well advised to dip into the various philosophies available. There are also many dimensions to colors. It would take a whole book in itself to explore the deeper meanings of colors. Therefore, I ask your indulgence while I simply provide you with sample meanings of a rainbow of colors.

I also encourage the exploration of colors through intuitive senses. For truly, it is through energetic communication that deeper feeling and understanding occurs for the color use of each individual. Each time I explore the colors surrounding a person I may find similar meaning to a color such as Violet; however, the individual will express that color in their own special way.

Color	Expressing As
Red	Passion, Power, Aggressiveness, Desire
Orange	Creativity, Innocence, Child-like Curiosity
Yellow	Joy, Clarity, Logic, Focus, Intent
Green	Love, Compassion, Imagination, Nurturing
Blue	Balance, Calmness, Intuition, Healing, Truth
Violet	Healing, Spiritual Intent, Humanitarianism

Table 13-1
Rainbow Correlations

Finally, we have a look at Diane McPherson's last spoke on her sacred path. Though simplified in Figure 13-1 below, the colors tell us quite a lot. We can associate information from the table of rainbow correlations and obtain a wider view-point of energy and activity in Diane's ability to manifest, heal and express her personal power.

In manifesting, Diane is at her best when she uses conscious intent (yellow) together with creative imagination (green). Her healing is best supported when she balances her life and listens to her intuitive voice direct her steps toward well-being. As we look at her Self Power we know that when she walks the path of her Spiritual journey she is strengthened. When she aligns with her humanitarian qualities she is powerful. When in her power she provides spiritual healing qualities to herself, loved ones, and the world.

Color Assistance

Colors:
Manifesting—Yellow/Green
Healing—Blue
Self Power—Violet

Challenge: An inability to heal, manifest, and express your personal power.

Way Out: Wear these colors, meditate on them, keep then in your line-of-sight. Balance your right/left brain (yellow/green), be gentle and spiritual in your knowing (blue and violet).

Figure 13-1
The Kaleidoscope of Diane

Your Rainbow Qualities

Look about you. What colors do you see most dominant in your life? Reds? Violets? Do you have a favorite color? How do you feel when you wear certain colors or sit within a room with a particular color that you like or don't like?

Colors are indeed life-enhancers. The colors that seem to provide you with the most positive response are likely the colors your soul has chosen for your spectrum of life enhancement. Also true is the fact that colors you dislike are supporting colors. Your dislike may simply be resistance to your inner power.

When you create your sacred space for meditation on your color spectrum, bring with you swatches of color. Center yourself. Become quiet and receptive. One by one pick up a color swatch. Feel its energy as it connects with you. When a color doesn't seem to provide you with any feeling, set it aside. Continue to work with the swatches that created a sensation while touching them and looking at them.

Next, handle the swatches with a question. How do you make me feel? Do you make me feel balanced? Do you make me feel powerful? Do you make me feel creative?

When you find the color that makes you feel balanced you have found your healing color. When you feel powerful, you have discovered your color of personal power. When you feel creative you have found your manifesting color.

These colors can now be consciously used by you. When you want to enhance healing, wear your healing color. When you meditate, visualize the healing color permeating the whole of you. Let your soul know that your are ready to be the conscious partner of the event of healing. Do the same with your manifesting color and self-power color.

After one client received her wheel and discovered that orange was her manifesting color she immediately used it in meditation to bring her abundance. She also brought the color out into her world with scarves that she wore. At the end of the week she purchased a lottery ticket and won $90.00. Just luck? No, use of energy that was more appropriately aligned with her.

CHAPTER 14

STARS AND PLANETS

Astrology

Throughout this book I have given hints of astrology. The study of this philosophy is another correlation of the energies the soul uses to enable its journey through the physical plane to be successful.

Astrology is an ancient science that observes the heavens and the alignment of stars and planets at the time of an individual's birth. Twelve zodiacal configurations are examined and decreed to emanate an energy that affects the personality of an individual when interacting with planetary influences. Ten planets energetically rule the astrological signs. Table 2-1 gives a brief description of the twelve zodiacal configurations and the ruling planet.

For the purpose of charting the soul intelligence, the astrological elements of importance are the position of constellations in conjunction with the sun, the moon, and the eastern horizon (known as the ascendant in astrology). At the moment of birth the energies from the entire cosmos radiate toward the Earth at a certain slant and meet at a certain angle in relationship to the individual. The angle of the sun represents "the main expression of the individual, the inner self and the inner personality. It is the heart of the chart." (Marion D. March & Joan McEvers, 1989:51.) The angle of the moon represents "emotions, instincts, moods, urges and desires."(1989:52). While the eastern horizon, known as the ascendant, reveals the "outer personality; how people see you and your physical appearance." (1989:52)

ZODIAC	DESCRIPTION	PLANET	DESCRIPTION
Aries	Dynamic/ Active	Mars	Initiative/ Aggressive
Taurus	Stable/ Practical	Venus	Social/ Affectionate
Gemini	Versatile/ Clever	Mercury	Intellectual/ Communicative
Cancer	Devotional/ Domestic	Moon	Intuitive/ Moody
Leo	Idealistic/ Ambitious	Sun	Power urge/ Leadership
Virgo	Practical/ Well-being	Mercury	Intellectual/ Communicative
Libra	Balance/ Companionship	Venus	Social/ Affectionate
Scorpio	Intensive/ Probing	Pluto	Transforming/ Reforming
Sagittarius	Philosophical/ Enthusiastic	Jupiter	Expansive/ Benevolent
Capricorn	Ambitious/ Responsible	Saturn	Discipline/ Limitations
Aquarius	Imaginative/ Independent	Uranus	Science/ Freedom
Pisces	Introspective/ Secret Knowing	Neptune	Intuition/ Illusion

Table 14-1
Basic Zodiac and Planetary Descriptions

Throughout the research of Sacred Path Wheels, associations were made by correlating an astrological chart of the individual to the information derived through each spoke of the wheel. Most particularly, interest was concentrated on the angle of the sun, the moon and the eastern horizon at the time the person was born. Strong interrelationships with stars and planets were also noted. For instance, if two or more planets were aligned with a zodiacal arrangement (such as Mars and Venus aligned with Gemini), a stronger energetic influence was noted. However, the sun, moon, and ascendant were the main focus. The question in mind was always, "How does this information confirm the information within the wheel and how does it support the process?" Correlations about personality traits and colors were made between the astrological chart and the Sacred Path Wheel. Frequently the spiritual guardian, the animal, plant, and mineral nature revealed in the Sacred Path Wheel had direct association with the zodiacal information of the person being charted.

In the book, *Initiations,* it is declared that human, animal, vegetable, and mineral energies aptly connect the Universal essence to all living things through the cosmic forces of the planets and stars. "Just like all the celestial bodies, the Earth represents the materialization of these various radiations, and that's why for each step of Earthly creation there is a form of materialization which primarily manifests the specific energy of the great cosmic wheel appropriate for the form of materialization concerned. That is to say that in rock formations, minerals, plants, animals and human beings here on Earth there are the materialized radiations of each individual constellation of the zodiac, as well as for each individual planet. ...When you see a lion, for example, you should remember that on the animal plane he is the materialized radiation of the particular zodiacal sign we call *"Leo"* or *"Lion"*. But at the same time there are minerals, plants and people made up of the same energy..." (Haich, 1974:256.)

Many associations can be given to the planetary alignments that exist at the time of a person's birth. It is recognized that the alignment of the stars and planets at the time of birth was a soul choice for further assistance in enhancing the goal of a life lesson.

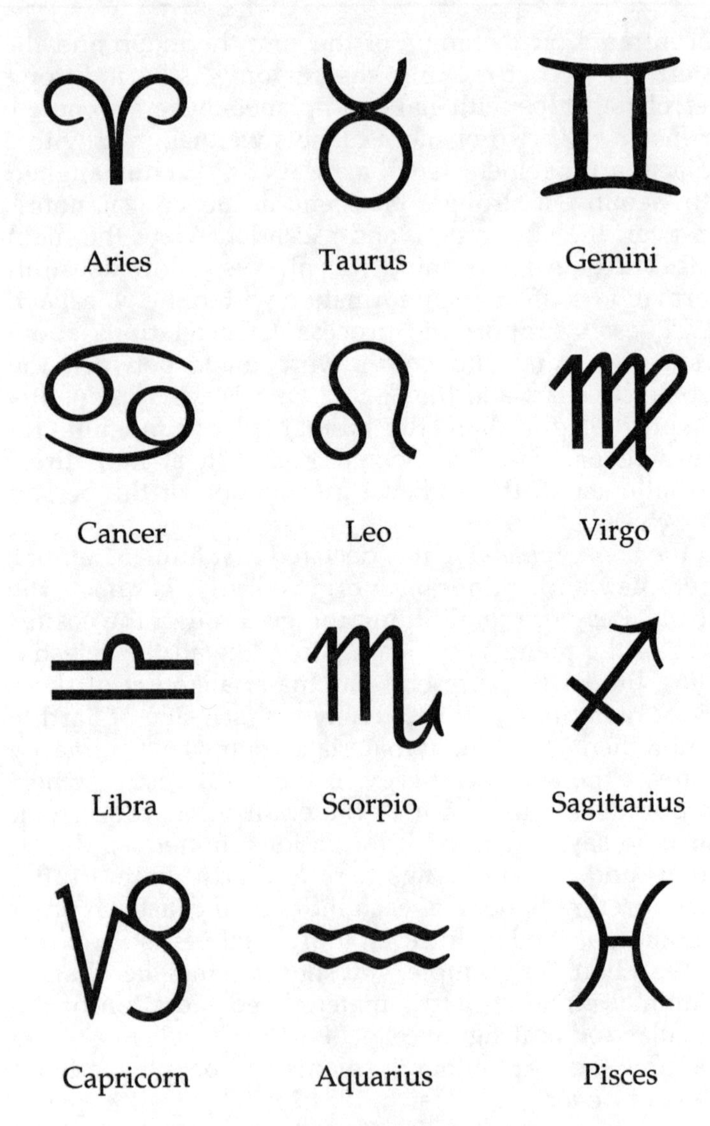

Table 14-2
Astrological Signs

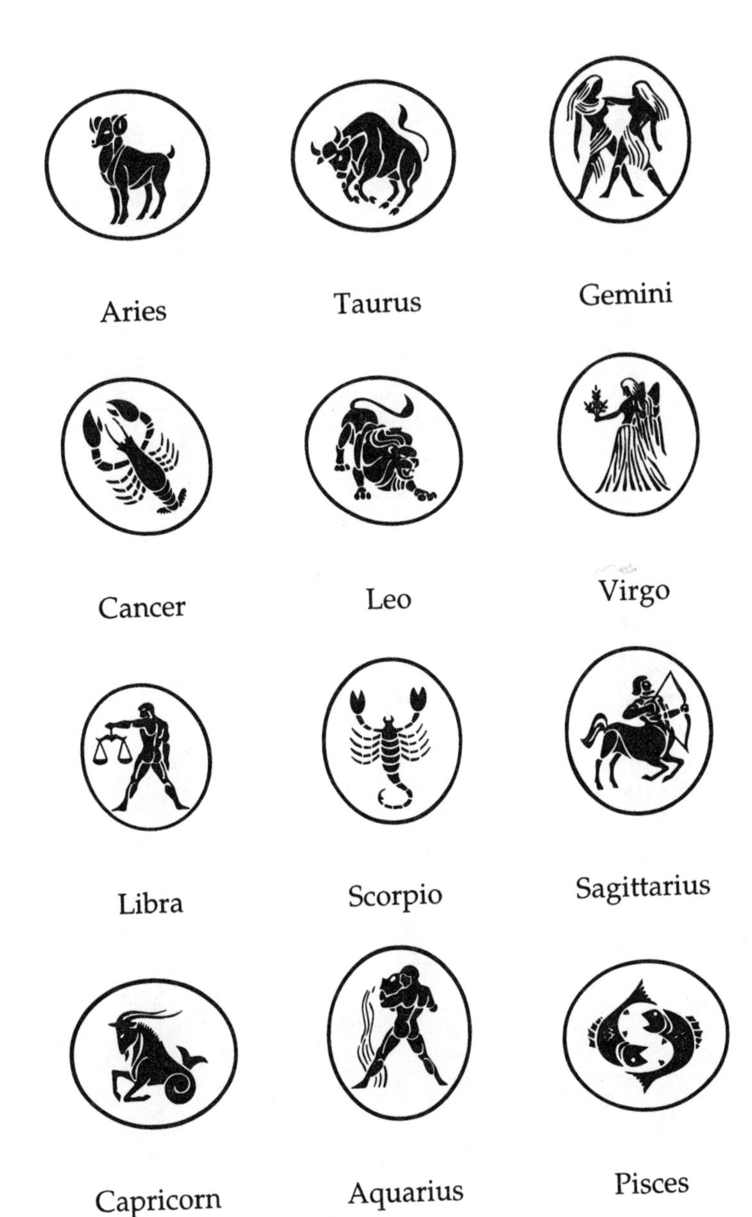

Table 14-3
Astrological Totems

CHAPTER 15

GATHERING IN GROUPS

Group Consciousness

As we have looked at the individual process, it is important to note that the Sacred Path Wheel© chart provides a map of the intelligence of the soul. It reveals the energy a soul accesses in order to follow the purpose of its life lesson. The energy is revealed as an alliance with spiritual guidance, instinctive and intuitive knowing, and the ability to adapt and grow through a physical existence. Additionally, the soul accesses the treasures of a given name to enhance a life pattern while expressing a personality to the outer world. Likewise, cherished relationships with others and gifting a unique essence of the personality to other human beings enhances the journey of the soul through a given life-time. As a personality progresses to higher levels of inner truth s/he radiates and accesses the lights of healing, manifesting and the power of self-expression. All of this keeps the personality in balance with the Universal Laws s/he may follow throughout an incarnation and aids in the completion of a goal—the life lesson.

Group intelligence may also be justifiably ascertained by further correspondences of Sacred Path Wheels©. More studies will have to occur in order to authenticate this concept. However, the apparent reflection of this idea came through the evaluation of the Sacred Path Wheels utilized for this study.

After reviewing many Sacred Path Wheel© charts the revelation in the form of group consciousness became noticeable. In relating one wheel to another it was apparent that more than one person carried the same animal nature, or spiritual guardian or even the same gift to humanity. Other similarities became evident as well. This created a question about possible soul-group associations. Could groups of souls be operating within the same energy framework to achieve collective gatherings and swifter union with the Whole? Are there such things as soul groups at all? What is their greater purpose? This I realize is another thesis. However, a brief look could be beneficial and will provide an inkling of soul group consciousness. Table 15-1 provides a partial listing of individual charts and correlations to their life lesson.

This table has two variables for you to work from to obtain the greatest use of the information being shared. (1) For each personal line of data, a number is presented. All fields of knowledge presented in the Sacred Path Wheel spokes are provided. Due to space limitations, only a few line items per page can be printed. Therefore, to follow the complete 12-spoke data for number 1, you must read both facing pages. The same applies for number 2, and so on. (2) The codes used in the table are at the end.

In Table 15-1 there are seven individuals who have utilized the Dolphin energy to assist their instinctual nature. Other correlations reveal they have similar reasons for being here, to achieve discovery, strength, sensitivity and futuristic developments. All but one called on the direction of the east to support their enlightenment process.

In the large cat family there were also several individuals who used this energetic field for their instinctual nature. Two of those individuals had the same spiritual guide, the same laws to follow, incorporated the east as part of their directional energy, and utilized similar color frequencies for their manifesting, health and self power.

In almost every case where the Archangel Haniel was called out the person's gift to humanity was to teach. In fact, in the discourse about Haniel and the order of angels that work with him (the Elohim), it is noted that they are given the task of assisting teachers and leaders.

Certainly we can see the differences in each sacred path chart. If everything was the same from one human being to another we would have little uniqueness and no variety. However, the similarities do bring up a question. Do groups of souls enter this Earth realm? If so why?

The study of soul intelligence is fascinating and never ending. Charting through the Sacred Path Wheel© is certainly a way to discover soul intelligence. The Sacred Path Wheel © also offers a way in which an individual can consciously know of their path and work toward their goal with clarity. Clarity opens the door to a stronger relationship with the Creator of all life and the union each soul desires as a Oneness.

	Lesson	Guide	Identity	Animal	Plant	Stone	Direction[1]
1	Experience strength of self	Chasmalim	11/9/2, Justice, Hermit, High Priestess	Opossum	Juniper	Abalone	A,W,N
2	Discover New Abilities	Elohim	2/3/5, High Priestess, Empress, Hierophant	Dolphin	Sage	Emerald	N,S,E,W
3	Know Your Vision	Raphael	7/4/11, Chariot, Emperor, Justice	Rodent	St. John's Wart	Copper	E,W
4	Learn about Nurturing	Ashim	6/7/4, Lovers, Chariot, Emperor	Buffalo	Lavender	Turquoise	A,B,E
5	Work with the Mind	Raphael	11/10/3, Justice, Wheel of Fortune, Empress	Dolphin	Saffron	Garnet	N,S,E
6	Open your mind & recognize self	Ratziel	10/7/8, Wheel of Fortune, Chariot, Strength	Red Fox	Lotus	Ruby	E,S
7	Expansion of Self	Sandalphon	5/3/8, Hierophant, Empress, Strength	White Horse	Prickly Ash Bark	Lapis Lazuli	A,W

Table 15-1 Dissection of Sacred Path Wheels© to Show Group Relationship

	Law(s)[2]	Intuit	Relationships	Gift	Color[3]
1	SL, NL, HL	Flash of Insight	Patience, Perseverance & Foresight	Creative Inspiration	M = Y H = BV S = V
2	NL, HL	Inquisitive/Futuristic	Relate with care and awareness	Bring in New ideas for Technology	M = YG H = Y S = RV
3	NL, HL	Free	Signals for change	Assist in Trusting Great Spirit	M = YO H = P S = BV,G
4	SL, HL	Quick, Impulsive, & Transforming	Interact without Expectations	Share Knowledge & wisdom with a loving nature	M = R H = YG S = V
5	SL, NL	Sensitive to deep feelings	Adapt, with Humility to changes	Open Heart	M = O H = G S = I, EB
6	SL, NL	Reflective	Creatively express wholeness by knowing the boundaries of each individual approach to life	Share what you know re wholistic healing	M = YO H = G S = V
7	SL, NL	Free, Curious & Connected to Greater Mind	Commitment brings rewards	Beautify & Enrich others	M = R,Y H = BG S = B

Table 15-1 Dissection of Sacred Path Wheels© to Show Group Relationship

	Lesson	Guide	Identity	Animal	Plant	Stone	Direction
8	Move Beyond Defense, Trust	Elohim	10/8/9, Wheel of Fortune, Strength, Hermit	Ant	Indian Root	Agate	S
9	Connect with True Source; Move through obstacles	Kuan Yin	11/7/9, Justice, Chariot, Hermit	Lizard	Hawthorne	Rose Quartz	A,W
10	Find Strength to move beyond fears	Seraphim	1/3/4, Magician, Empress, Emperor	Buffalo	Grapes	Abalone	E,W,B
11	Nurturing self and others thru love	Auriel	6/8/5, Lovers, Strength, Hierophant	Dolphin	Sassafras	Lapidalite	A,B,N,E,S, W
12	Move beyond struggle as an individual	Raphael, Beni Elohim	7/8/6, Chariot, Strength, Lovers	Cougar	White Lily	Rose Quartz	E,W
13	Cover the burdens of the heart by under-standing	Tzadkiel	8/10/9, Strength, Wheel of Fortune, Hermit	Scarab	Parsley	Red Jasper	A,B,N
14	Move always towards a goal	Tzaphkiel	3/5/8, Empress, Hierophant, Strength	Rhino, Panther	Plantain	Moonstone	A,B,E

Table 15-1 Dissection of Sacred Path Wheels© to Show Group Relationship

	Law(s)	Intuit	Relationships	Gift	Color
8	NL, HL	Blended Consciousness	Breakthroughs to Personal Understanding	Reveal Potentials	M = RV H = BV S = V
9	SL, NL	Listen to Inner Teacher	Power as a communicator and healer	Fertility & new beginnings	M = B H = OG S = Y,V
10	NL, HL	Strength & ability to communicate with True Spirit	Growth thru strength, love and understanding	Assist others to obtain balance in Physical	M = Y H = G S = B
11	SL	Mystical knowledge thru nature	Maintain Uniqueness while uniting	Be sensitive, loving and share deep knowing	M = G,Y H = Pi,L S = Y,B
12	SL, NL, HL	Swift desire and patience	Journey thru trust	Balance while moving forward with power, focus and desire	M = Y H = BV S = SB
13	NL, HL	Balanced reflection of True Will	Healing forces thru creativity	Reflect true nature of others	M = YO H = B S = V
14	SL,NL, HL	Prophetic insight	Agreement to focus on truth	Freedom to express their true selves	M = YO H = G S = Y/B

Table 15-1 Dissection of Sacred Path Wheels© to Show Group Relationship

	Lesson	Guide	Identity	Animal	Plant	Stone	Direction
15	Gain Your Identity	Haniel, Elohim	11/3/5, Justice, Empress, Hierophant	Night Eagle (owl)	Hops Jade	Green	A,W,B
16	Come from Truth	Aralim	1/3/4, Magician, Empress, Emperor	Coyote, Bear	Passion Flower	Diamond	S,N,W
17	Be connected to earth as a catalyzer	Tzaphkiel	8/5/4, Strength, Hierophant, Emperor	Horned Owl	Jasmine	Blue Lace Agate	B,E
18	Clear mind, Clear speaking	Haniel	3/3/6, Empress, Lovers	Lizard	Tuberose	Moonstone	N,S,E,B
19	Break pattern of silence to experience new state of being	Michael	1/10/11, Magician, Wheel of Fortune, Justice	Beaver	Beech	Imperial Jasper	E,W
20	Understand forces of Life	Tzaphkiel	1/8/9, Magician, Strength, Hermit	Dolphin/ Whale	Chamomile	Jet/Hematite	W,N,B
21	Connect with True Inner Self	Raphael	11/7/9, Justice, Chariot, Hermit	Sea Otter	Echinacea	Clear Quartz	A,N

Table 15-1 Dissection of Sacred Path Wheels© to Show Group Relationship

	Law(s)	Intuit	Relationships	Gift	Color
15	SL, NL	Speak what you hear from within	Listen to needs by feeling them	Teach others how to move thru life	M = R,G H = YG S = RV
16	SL, NL	Abundant, creative	Gateway to self understanding	Assist others to aspire to true power	M = B H = O S = G
17	NL, HL	Creative visions	Let go of control and trust the process	Inspire thru arts/theater	M = B H = G,B S = G,Y,B
18	SL	Quick, Mind to mouth	Gift of freedom	Be an oracle	M = G H = B S = Y
19	NL, HL	Listening, connecting & trusting	Seek wisdom, understanding and companionship	Recognize importance of individuality	M = G H = BV S = Y,G
20	SL, NL, HL	Aligned with Earth Mother	Fertile thru changes and harmony	Teach what you know	M = BG H = G,R S = B, G
21	SL, HL	Quickened by Desire	Enhanced through Mindfulness	Transition	M = YG H = YO S = Y

Table 15-1 Dissection of Sacred Path Wheels© to Show Group Relationship

	Lesson	Guide	Identity	Animal	Plant	Stone	Direction
22	Become one with Many	Sandalphon	3/10/4, Empress, Wheel of Fortune, Emperor	Raven	Mullein	Carnelian	W, N, S
23	Accept peace Internally & Externally	Chasmalim	3/8/11, Empress, Strength, Justice	Red Cardinal	White wild rose	White Calcite	A,B, E, W
24	Reflect light of True Source	Khamael	6/7/4, Lovers, Chariot, Emperor	Bull	Angelica	Bloodstone	A, E
25	Know when to speak and when to be silent	Sandalphon	9/7/7, Hermit, Chariot	Blue Jay	Raspberry	Green Jasper	A,B,E,W
26	To know joy and peace	Kerubim	2/5/7, High Priestess, Hierophant, Chariot	Otter	Grains	Green Adventurine	A,B,E,W
27	Move beyond isolation & seriousness to playfulness	Beni Elohim	10/3/4, Wheel of Fortune, Empress,Emperor	Mtn. Lion	Wild Yam	Gold	N,E
28	Don't do it so hard	Malachim	10/9/10, Wheel of Fortune, Hermit	Wolf,crow	Black Cohosh	Ruby	E,N,S

Table 15-1 Dissection of Sacred Path Wheels© to Show Group Relationship

	Law(s)	Intuit	Relationships	Gift	Color
22	SL, NL	Clairsentient	Balanced through boundary setting	Teach others to explore new Horizons	M = R H = RV S = B
23	NL, HL	Clairsentient	Patience, understanding	Generosity	M = R H = O S = B
24	SL, NL, HL	Innocence & open-mindedness	Cultivate, harvest through patience	Playfully show the way to new beginings	M = B H = O S = G
25	SL, HL	Clairvoyant	A foundation for transformation	Listen and counsel	M = YG H = SB S = I,Y
26	SL, NL	Channel for Universal info	Clarity & willingness to change	Patience, compassion and Unconditional love	M = RV H = G S = YG
27	SL, NL, HL	Hear/Feel	Interact with clarity	Work with hands	M = YG H = B S = V
28	SL,NL,HL	Trusting & Spontaneous	Evolve without over evaluation	Illuminate Self Power of others	M = G H = G S = R,Pi

Table 15-1 Dissection of Sacred Path Wheels© to Show Group Relationship

	Lesson	Guide	Identity	Animal	Plant	Stone	Direction
29	Hear correctly, speak truth	Ratziel	5/9/5, Hierophant, Hermit	Black bear	Blueberry	Snowflake Obsidian	N
30	Be passionate about your existence	Metatron	6/4/10, Lovers, Emperor, Wheel of Fortune	Snake	Kelp	Amethyst	A,E
31	Open Heart	Auriel	9/10/10, Hermit, Wheel of Fortune	Night Eagle (owl)	Comfrey	Malachite	A,E,
32	Respect for All	Tzadkiel	8/7/6, Strength, Chariot, Lovers	Eagle	Holly	Green Tourmaline	A,B
33	Know and earn your knowing	Beni Elohim	1/10/11, Magician, Wheel of Fortune, Justice	Red-tailed Hawk	Pine & Pine nuts	Copper	N,S
34	Clear intentions	Hecate	10/6/7 Wheel of Fortune, Lovers, Chariot	Dolphin	Dong Quai	Bloodstone	A,B
35	Stay focused and directed to make clear decisions	Michael	2/2/4, High Priestess, Emperor	Spider	Yarrow	Bloodstone	E,A,S

Table 15-1 Dissection of Sacred Path Wheels© to Show Group Relationship

	Law(s)	Intuit	Relationships	Gift	Color
29	SL, HL	Clairvoyant	Freedom from constraints	Share wisdom	M = R H = YG S = BV
30	SL, NL	Inner/Outer reflection	Gateway to further understanding	Share passion for life	M = V H = BG S = Y
31	SL, NL, HL	Listening to inner teacher	Joy thru understanding	Use ability to communicate	M = YG H = B S = Y
32	SL, NL	Connected to Christ Consciousness	Eliminate resistance	Heal with spiritual integrity	M = G H = BV S = Pi
33	SL, NL, HL	Knowing	Opportunities for growth	Changes of mind thru true knowledge	M = G H = B/P S = P
34	SL, HL	Spontaneous	Transformational	Regenerate spirit thru emotional understanding	M = Y,R H = BG S = T,P
35	NL, HL	Auditory	Communicate thru talking & listening	Teach expansion	M = RO H = BV S = Y

Table 15-1 Dissection of Sacred Path Wheels© to Show Group Relationship

	Lesson	Guide	Identity	Animal	Plant	Stone	Direction
36	Be aware and alert	Khamael	11/5/7, Justice, Hierophant, Chariot	Panther	Grape	Sodalite	N,S,E,W
37	Use wisdom you carry	Tzaphkiel	7/9/7, Chariot, Hierophant	Snake	Bayberry	Moonstone	A,B,W
38	Purify bindings that keep you from knowing	Ashim	10/1/11 Wheel of Fortune, Magician, Justice	Coyote	Fern	Moonstone	N,S,E,W
39	Use self love and self determination to move beyond complacency	Sandalphon, Goddess Ceres	1/11/3, Magician, Justice, Empress	Raven	Hyacinth	Sodalite	A,B,N
40	Expansion thru teaching	Elohim, Haniel	6/3/9, Lovers, Empress, Hermit	Wolf	Marshmallow	Malachite	E,W,N,S
41	Communicate Truth	Uriel	2/4/6, High Priestess, Emperor, Lovers	Buffalo	Mulberry bush	Petrified wood	A,B,N
42	Understanding, living, and nurturing	Khamael	3/4/7, Empress, Emperor, Chariot	Spider	Vine	Chrysocolla	N,S,E,W

Table 15-1 Dissection of Sacred Path Wheels© to Show Group Relationship

	Law(s)	Intuit	Relationships	Gift	Color
36	SL, NL	Sensitive	Communicate from inside to outside	Teach	M = R H = B S = BV
37	SL, NL	Transmitive Channel	Connections that reflect wisdom	Speak and Teach	M = O H = B,S S = I
38	NL, HL	Flows from space of sacred knowing	Harmonized through balance of physical and spiritual	Be of spiritual service	M = I H = Pi S = B
39	NL, HL	Silent knowing thru mental balance	Immerse yourself in experience of relating	Gather and share knowledge	M = G H = G S = BV
40	HL	Alignment with Earth Mother	Spiritually sensitive	Knowledge shared	M = G H = R,Y,G S = Y,I
41	NL	Illuminating and joyful	Open and revealing without effort	Provide intuitive knowing to create equilibrium	M = Y H = V S = T
42	NL, HL	Clairvoyant	Understand differences	Teach	M = R,Y H = YG S = R,Y

Table 15-1 Dissection of Sacred Path Wheels© to Show Group Relationship

	Lesson	Guide	Identity	Animal	Plant	Stone	Direction
43	Have clear and decisive knowing	Holy Living Creatures	8/5/4, Strength, Hierophant, Emperor	Whale, dolphin	Hyacinth	Lace Agate	A,B,E
44	To be stable	Maiden who becomes a bear	11/2/4, Justice, High Priestess, Emperor	Porcupine	Gentian	Lace Agate	A,B
45	Honor your position in life	Metatron	5/6/7, Hierophant, Lovers, Chariot	Dolphin	Aconite	Snowflake Obsidian	A,E
46	Bridge emotions to consciousness	Uriel	1/3/4, Magician, Empress, Emperor	Snake	Grains	Bloodstone	E,S,A
47	Be alert to transform	Michael	1/7/8, Magician, Chariot, Strength	Snow dog	Licorice	Gold	N,E,S
48	Trust	Ratziel	7/8/6, Chariot, Strength, Lovers	Bear	Yellow rose	Turquoise	S,E
49	Return to loving awareness	Aralim	6/9/6, Lovers, Hermit	Lizard	Water Reed	Amethyst	W,E,S

Table 15-1 Dissection of Sacred Path Wheels© to Show Group Relationship

	Law(s)	Intuit	Relationships	Gift	Color
43	SL, HL	Clairsentient, Clairvoyant	Resolving karmic patterns	Reveal the power of a clear mind	M = YO H = G S = B
44	HL, NL	Wisdom thru feeling	Review with reflection	Teacher of wisdom, spiritual search	M = YG H = B S = I
45	NL	Quietly observing	Initiate relationships	Teach with loving counsel	M = Y H = R S = B
46	SL, NL, HL	Psychically energetic	Growth thru adjustments	Serve humanity with love	M = G H = V S = BV
47	SL, NL, HL	Swift spiritual sensations	Joy, open heart, patience	Wisdom	M = Y H = BG S = YG
48	SL	Magical knowing	Possessiveness vs. Freedom	Openly use creative & intuitive gifts	M = O H = BG S = Y,R
49	SL, NL	Impulsive & transforming	Assist the return to love	Love thru synthesizing knowledge	M = Y H = YO S = BV

Table 15-1 Dissection of Sacred Path Wheels© to Show Group Relationship

	Lesson	Guide	Identity	Animal	Plant	Stone	Direction
50	Empowerment through moderation	Malachim	5/3/8, Hierophant, Empress, Strength	Lion, dolphin	Lady	Amethyst	A,E
51	Go beneath surface	Sandalphon	4/3/7, Emperor, Empress, Chariot	Dolphin	Angelica	Obsidian	S,E
52	Seek Truth	Haniel	1/3/4, Magician, Empress, Emperor	Opossum	Elder	Chrysocolla	E,N
53	Decisions	Beni Elohim	10/3/4 Wheel of Fortune, Empress, Emperor	Crow	Lady's Mantle	White Calcite	A,W
54	Heal and move into wholeness	Ashim	4/8/3 Emperor, Strength, Empress	Dragon	Yarrow	Black Onyx	A,B,N
55	Know your Will to connect with True Will	Auphanim	5/7/3, Hierophant, Chariot, Empress	Red-tailed Hawk	Kelp	Chrysocolla	E,N, S
56	Move boy to man and man to boy	Seraphim	10/7/8, Wheel of Fortune, Chariot, Strength	Red Snake	Jade	Strawberry quartz	A,B,N,E

Table 15-1 Dissection of Sacred Path Wheels© to Show Group Relationship

	Law(s)	Intuit	Relationships	Gift	Color
50	SL, NL	Balance of Body, Mind, and Spirit	Harmonizing and modifying	Clarity, understanding, and truth	M = B H = Y S = V
51	SL, HL	Strong, connection with True Spirit	Initiate relationships	Bring them thru oppression	M = Y H = YG S = Y,B
52	NL, HL	Guided by Universal Energies	Trust, surrender, relinquish control	Assist others to move on	M = Y H = BG S = BV
53	NL, HL	Innocence and trust	Movement through progressive changes	Understanding and intuitive reflection	M = C H = YG S = B
54	NL, HL	Strong when connected to Earth Mother	Weaving, connecting and setting boundaries	Listen, guide to truth and reality of Higher Presence	M = YG H = BG S = B,V
55	SL, NL	Clairvoyant, Clairsentient	Share and relate to those of similar nature	Listen, speak, teach	M = Pi H = BV S = Y
56	SL	Strong when connected to cycles of life	Opportunities to experience friends and teachers	Reveal knowing through internal records	M = B H = I S = R

Table 15-1 Dissection of Sacred Path Wheels© to Show Group Relationship

	Lesson	Guide	Identity	Animal	Plant	Stone	Direction
57	Understanding cycles of life	Aralim	7/9/7, Chariot, Hermit	Rhino	Wood Betony	Ruby	A,B
58	Depart from Aloneness	Tzadkiel	7/9/7, Chariot, Hermit	Dolphin	Squawvine	Quartz	A,E,S
59	Walk this earth in joy	Raphael	1/11/3, Magician, Justice, Empress	Eagle	Licorice, Spearmint	Garnet, Turquoise	A.B
60	Utilize energy of Divine Creator to change	Khamael	2/5/7, High Priestess, Hierophant, Chariot	Scorpion	Vervain	Turquoise	A,E,W
61	Honor emotions and sensitivity	Khamael	3/10/4, Empress, Wheel of Fortune, Emperor	Lion/ Lioness	Marijuana	Quartz	A,B,E

Table 15-1 Dissection of Sacred Path Wheels© to Show Group Relationship

	Law(s)	Intuit	Relationships	Gift	Color
57	SL, NL	Sensitive to Deep Feelings	Commitment	Teach from heart	M = YO H = YG S = B
58	SL, NL	Visionary	Go Beyond external expectations	Teach	M = RO H = YO S = B
59	SL, NL	Eyes beyond eyes	Listen with patience and foresight	Brilliance of mind and birthing of new ideas	M = RO H = G,R S = V
60	SL, NL	Sensitive	Learn to balance emotions	Loving expression of self	M = V H = YO S = R
61	SL, HL	Mystical	Flow into growth and awareness	Teach spiritual aspects of physical	M = I H = B S = V,Y

Table 15-1 Dissection of Sacred Path Wheels© to Show Group Relationship

Codes for Table 15-1 Dissection of Sacred Path Wheels© to Show Group Relationship

[1]Direction Codes	
Code	**Direction**
A	Above
B	Below
W	West
N	North
E	East
S	South

[2]Law Codes	
Code	**Law(s)**
SL	Sacred Law
NL	Natural Law
HL	Human Law

[3]Color Type Codes	
Code	**Type**
M	Manifesting
H	Healing
S	Self Power

[3]Color Codes	
Code	**Color**
B	Blue
BG	Blue Green
BV	Blue Violet
C	Crimson
EB	Electric Blue
G	Gold
G	Green
I	Indigo
L	Lilac
O	Orange
OG	Olive Green
P	Purple
Pi	Pink
R	Red
RO	Red Orange
RV	Red Violet
SB	Silver Blue
T	Turquoise
V	Violet
Y	Yellow
YG	Yellow Green
YO	Yellow Orange

CHAPTER 16

DISCUSSION

Throughout this book we have noted correlations of mineral, plant animal, human, and spiritual natures and presented metaphysical interpretations. It is truly through understanding correlations that the interconnection with all life is seen. Correlations provide a magical language that offers insight into hidden realities that, perhaps, could not be grasped by the human intellect. Awe-inspiring intelligence is revealed through these associations. It has been seen over and over that this wisdom or intelligence supports a goal. Through the Sacred Path Wheels it is seen that the intelligence was used to achieve completion of a life lesson. Repeatedly, the intelligent factor of choice brought forward energetic alliance with Universal forces that would aid in building, living, and completing a life-cycle. Again we may ask, "What intelligence integrates such potential energy for the achievement of a goal?"

I believe that the soul intelligence is the acting force. Certainly it is motivated by the Higher Power of the Great Creator. However, each individual soul has been given a Free Will. Throughout many sessions of channeling the Free Will of the soul expressed itself with desire to collect the facets necessary to establish a pattern of living. This pattern allows a given personality an opportunity to learn lessons necessary for an incarnation. It was also apparent that the soul has a greater goal: to know the WHOLE, the

Oneness of the Universe. Soul dialogue in channeling sessions reveals that every incarnation is a gathering of more and more information until ALL is known and the return to the Great Creator is accomplished.

Further Review of Charts

To provide an understanding of the consistent information of soul intelligence as noted through the Sacred Path Wheel©, two other individual's wheels are introduced. Review this material with this question in mind: "How does it all correlate?" Also ask, "What do the consistencies reveal?" Do you experience the incredible feeling of the awesomeness of soul intelligence?

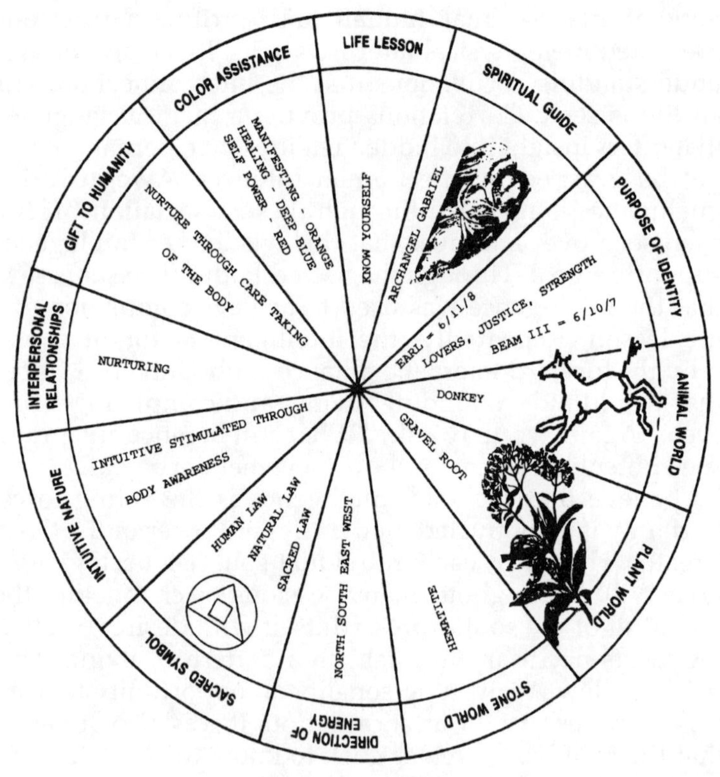

Figure 16-1
Earl Beam's Sacred Path Wheel©

Life Lesson: *Know yourself through physical connection.* Throughout this life experience you are to connect with your body and emotions in order to know yourself. That connection will allow you to get to know who you truly are. Self identification allows you to move beyond fears, experience your desires as manifestations, and face what you need to know in this life time.

Challenge: When you do not know yourself you will find yourself floundering, stubborn, and selfish. You will feel as though you are on a constant search for strength and perfection. Your motive for movement will be fear. You will try to take control over your position and the position of others. This will be due to feelings of insecurities and misplaced ego alignment.

Way Out: Go into your feelings and come to an understanding of who you truly are, what you want and why you want it. Move beyond your fears of the need to be in control of events and circumstances. Take action by activating your body awareness. Be conscious of the messages your body gives you. Whenever you find yourself holding back from anything begin asking yourself the question, "What have I to fear?" Then be willing to feel the fear message. Once you know what it is—give it away and move into your true sense of higher power and self-knowing.

Spiritual Guide: *Archangel Gabriel.* (Interesting to note here that Gabriel is the angelic ruler of the month of January.) Gabriel rules over the emotional and physical processes. It is through these two levels that your Higher Self has chosen to be more clearly in touch with self. Gabriel helps you move into your body through emotional awareness. He helps you move beyond fears by teaching you what is locked in your subconscious or automatic mind. He provides you with strength to know your emotions, your soul-knowing, your power to speak and listen, and your power to reproduce. He will also help you utilize your intuitive powers and move with the cycles and phases of reality.

Challenge: When not utilizing your assistant, you may find yourself locked in fears or blocked from your deep inner knowing. The cycles and phases of life will become a roller coaster of discomfort. You will ignore your emotions and the warning voices of your Higher Self. You will not see yourself as you truly are. It is quite likely that you will find that you are in states of delusion and rationalization of your situations, circumstances and events of your life experiences. You will tend to rely on your logic instead of combining logic with intuitive processes. Repeated patterns of existence will occur and you may struggle with them. You will feel as though they have taken control over your life rather than you taking control and moving into the changes. It will be difficult to set new exciting patterns in your existence.
Way Out: Call on the Archangel Gabriel. Then listen through feeling. Allow yourself to connect with your subconscious mind and take charge of what goes in and through it so that you can reach a true sense of strength, knowing, and connection to your Higher Self. Through Gabriel you will know your true strength and true identity. Gabriel will teach you how to flow with the tides of life, connect with the power of your intuition, and to speak the truth of your inner knowing.

Identity: *Earl = 6/11/8 (Lovers, Justice, Strength).* Spiritually we see that you are to utilize communication as a form of connecting with your Higher Self. Communication can be both verbally and through meditation. Relationships are important to you in gaining an understanding of what this life experience is all about. Spiritually, you also bring forth an ability to heal (self and others). Mentally, education and knowing at higher levels is important to you. It helps you maintain balance, forthrightness, and clarity in the direction(s) you are going. Knowing all that you need to know before acting is also a part of your mental aspecting. Physically, the body is important. Physical strength and endurance is important in that it allows you to connect with your inner knowing. Your first name reveals the need to know, love, express love, and experience love in its

whole nature—its unconditional nature. It also exposes the need to keep all things in balance, beauty, and harmony.
Challenge: *Beam = 6/10/7 (Lovers, Wheel of Fortune, Chariot).* Keeping things together will often times frustrate you. You will find great challenges in relationships (both mentally and physically). You may find it difficult at times to express what you need to others. If things do not connect just right for you, you may decide to drift off in your thinking to grandiose ideas, mentally be too much into the future rather than in the now, and delude yourself rather than face realities. Your timing will be off. You will feel out-of-balance, and your ego will get in the way. You will also note that you will try to move too fast through something that requires your steadfast attention. This may, in fact, affect your physical attention and your ability to identify who you are in any given moment. You will not "feel" your experience, you will intellectualize it. Your intellectualizing will fall short of your true knowing. You will find yourself battling to win in a situation that requires you to put your battle gear down and come to a quiet resolve through a greater understanding.
Way Out: Stay connected at all times to all aspects of yourself—your mental, emotional, physical and spiritual alignment. Continue to allow yourself to learn the facts and realities of how one is to take dominion over his Earthly existence. Finish projects before you move onto new adventures. Take dominion over yourself through love and excitement over the living existences around you. Come to understand the Law of Cause and Effect and know that everything you think, speak and do comes back to you—choose what you want in your life. Above all, connect with your self identity through your alignment with your Higher Self. Then reach out to this physical existence with joy and excitement and a radiance of who you are.

Animal: *Donkey.* This animal reveals your nature to be one of strength, stamina, and an ability to carry your load as well as the load of others, when necessary. Instinctively you know when you must move and when you must stay.

You know how to carry your load in this life and how to be sure-footed about your walk through this incarnation. You can climb to great heights or move into the depths of yourself. Above all, you can stay grounded and connected to Earth mother and the physical reality for which you are a part.
Challenge: You will not be in positive alignment with your instincts when you are stubborn, unwilling to change or move, and unwilling to see the other side of any circumstance. You will refuse to carry your load (much less understand anyone else's). You will find yourself uncomfortable with the direction you are going and yet unable to clarify the best path to take. Your mind will begin to vacillate, your emotions will begin to frustrate you, and your body will just be tired and unwilling to move.
Way Out: Realign with your instinctual nature. Call on the nature spirit of the donkey. Move into your strength and stamina to get beyond obstacles in your path. Take it slow and easy. Balance the load that you carry—do not over do it. Let your instincts guide you and you will always be in the right place at the right time.

Plant: *Gravel Root*. This plant has a planetary alignment with Saturn and the zodiacal sign of Capricorn. It, in that alignment, will help you maintain your stamina and desire to grow through the connection with your physical existence versus trying to get too much into the mental and day-dream away your requirements for the present moment. All of this reveals that your growth and adaptive nature is one of staying connected to yourself and get to know who you are through your physical and intuitive realities. This plant root is used as a diuretic, stimulant, astringent, and nervine. It is known as a treatment for too much uric acid in the system. It is used in healing practices for such ailments as, headaches, hysteria, impotence, indigestion, sciatica, sore throat, urine retention, and vomiting (just to name a few).
Challenge: When not utilizing this energy of growth and adaptation you may find yourself ungrounded and undisciplined. You will be scattered. Your world and

environment will be chaotic. Making decisions will be difficult and communicating your needs will be next to impossible. You will find yourself tired, frustrated, jumpy, and unable to manifest what you desire.
Way Out: Align with this plant energy for soul-memory. Keep this plant in your line-of-sight. Utilize its healing qualities in teas or tinctures. Remember to relax in order to get to the center of your reality. Then, you can make clear decisions and know in which direction you should be going in order to be in alignment with your desires.

Stone: *Hematite.* This is a stone of Capricorn. The energy pattern of hematite grounds you and places you in clear alignment with your soul-knowing. Its color ranges from steel gray to red and black. The healer, Galen, used it for the eyes and for headaches. It was also used by other healers for blood disorders, and dangerous wounds. (Warriors used this stone because it was believed to assist them in being invulnerable.) It, too, is known to work with the kidneys (as is gravel root) by cleansing the blood. Your soul choice was to utilize this stone in keeping you aware of who you are in this physical incarnation. Hematite is a stone that is utilized to connect with past incarnations as well so that healing from that time may occur.
Challenge: When not utilizing this energy for strength and personal awareness, you will find yourself ungrounded and disassociated from self-awareness and disconnected from others. You may, in fact, experience headaches, small to large wounds, and toxic disorders. Because you will not be centered and aware, you will not reveal your power to yourself or others. Also, you will not be able to learn from past mistakes and may find yourself repeating unfavorable problems, habits, and circumstances.
Way Out: Carry this stone in your back pocket (its energy is best utilized when the stone is next to the base of the spine). Keep it in your line-of-sight. Call on the nature spirits of this stone world to give you insight and knowing about your strength, power and ability to stay alert and aware of your journey through this incarnation. Be willing to stay grounded and attentive to your moment-to-

moment activities. Stay in alignment with your physical body so it may provide you strength and stamina for continual growth and learning. Utilize this stone as a reflector so you may reveal your inner mind (subconscious knowing).

Directions: North, south, east, and west. These directions create the essence of grounding and understanding of one's self. They assist you in honoring the whole of you—your mental, emotional, physical, and spiritual beingness. They balance the ebb and flow, growth and adaptation, emotional clarity, and inner knowing.

Challenge: When not aligned with these energy fields as a whole, you may find yourself unbalanced, unclear, and ungrounded in your existence. You may experience a smugness one day, and a low self-esteem the next day. You may become frustrated with your physical existence, your physical body and feel unable to maintain a specific health program due to low energy or no stamina. You will find it difficult to rely on your inner wisdom, logic, or even your strength.

Way Out: Daily align with the energies of the north, south, east and west directions. Be willing to move into new experiences, grow with them, feel them, and gain a deeper understanding of them. Feel your strength, alignment with mother Earth, and desire to obtain a connection with self-understanding by recognizing the beauty of all life.

Symbol: Square within a triangle within a circle. You are here to work with and understand all laws—Human Law, Sacred Law, and Natural Law. You are to see your physical self as the center of your existence, and in alignment with your spiritual self while assisted to greater understanding through your natural self. Human law deals with the physical realities of your existence, your body, your Earthly government, and the laws of the land. It determines form and density, and social structure. It requires you to give honor to your physical existence. Human Law is the only law that is influenced by human concepts of order and logic. Therefore, it is changeable and transient. Sacred Law is considered the Law of Laws. It is the Law of Love. It rules the true nature of the Universe and encompasses all forms of existence. It is non-judgmental, constant, perfect and unchangeable. You connect with it by connecting with your spiritual self and your Creator. You acknowledge it by loving, appreciating, and finding beauty in all things. Natural Law reveals the continuous expansion and contraction of the Universe—evolution. It governs nature, time, cycles, seasons, birth and transformation.

Challenge: When not in alignment with these laws you will find yourself having difficulty in a wide-range of experiences. From Human Law you may find yourself struggling with strength and endurance of the human body. You will not nurture the body or your physical environment. You may find that you experience ailments. You will find that systems give you difficulty—computers, banks, schools, businesses, etc. You may be frustrated by laws set down by governmental agencies and other human-oriented agencies. You may, in fact, be involved with legal situations beyond your control. When disconnected from Sacred Law you will find yourself unloving and unloved, disassociated from your spiritual nature and God, your creator. You will not find the beauty in life nor the reasons for living in the physical realm as important lesson learning processes. If you disconnect from natural law, you will find yourself out-of-sync, and unable to connect with your own biorhythm. You will find your time is off. You will not be in time or on time for events that support you. The ebb and flow of life will be a struggle and the rewards will be few. Everything will seem like it is ending. New beginnings and new ideas will thwart you. Or, everything will seem like it is beginning but you cannot complete projects or meet opportunities for gain and adventure.

Way Out: Come to an understanding of these laws. Activate them into your conscious awareness daily. Connect with Great Spirit. Love all that life has to offer. See everything as Sacred. Take care of your physical realities. Stay grounded. Be respectful of all Earthly matters. Follow the laws of the land—if they are inappropriate, be willing to stand up for the cause to change them. Honor your body and the physical aspect of others. Be in alignment with cycles and phases of your life and nature. Whatever project is ready to be completed, complete it and let it go. Whatever is ready for a new beginning, begin it, develop it, grow with it, reap your rewards from it, complete it, then let it go. Be on time and in time for all things. Follow natures way. Understand seasons and how you can adapt body, mind and spirit to the seasons. Walk in alignment with Human Law, Sacred Law and Natural Law.

Your intuitive nature: *Intuitive stimulated through body awareness.* Your intuitive nature comes alive when you are in alignment with your physical body. When you know who you are in a grounded, clear way, with clarity and self-awareness, you connect to your inner knowing. You hear the inner voice of your Higher Self and can respond to life more fully.

Challenge: When disconnected from your body you will be disconnected from your intuitive self. Your body will be in discomfort and stress. You will find yourself spinning your wheels trying to stay physically and mentally alert and aware of True Knowing. You will be lethargic and frustrated with your mental unclarity and physical inabilities.

Way Out: Pay attention to the needs of your physical body. Nurture it. Temper it with the right types of food, rest, exercise, play and work. Relax and go within to hear the inner voice of knowing. It is at this point that your intuitive senses are sharpened, aligned, and clear directions can be heard within.

Relationships: *Nurturing.* You are to nurture and be nurtured by relationships. Through this action with others you will find yourself experiencing abundance through health, wealth, joy and Divine Influence. You will share good fortune and receive good fortune in all levels of your life. You will see the truth in the Universal acclaim that we are all one—you will feel it and know it.

Challenge: An inability to be nurtured or to nurture others. Frustration will take over. You will begin to fall short in your endeavors. You will not trust others and will be doubtful that situations involving others can bring you joy, abundance, or opportunities for growth. You will not be giving and supportive and will not see the wisdom in events where others have been your teacher or personal reflection of yourself.

Way Out: Treat all relationships in a respectful and nurturing fashion. Allow yourself the opportunity to be nurtured and respected by others. Be joyous in the life-sharing that occurs by experiencing circumstances, events and opportunities with others. Let Divine Influence show you the way to be one with all people in a loving, caring, sharing, nurturing manner. It is in this alignment that you will see the true reflection of yourself.

Gift to Humanity: *Nurture through the care taking of the body.* You have, and are gaining throughout this life time, the wisdom of the body. Knowing this, and nurturing the body you will connect to the True Self. This in turn is your gift to humanity. Teach others to connect to themselves through their bodies. Listen to the speaking that the body reveals for health, happiness, love, nurturing, and so forth.

Challenge: When not gifting to humanity you will find yourself disconnected from knowledge, disconnected from true understanding, and unable to feel and heal. Your body wisdom will fall short of reality. You will not express yourself with clarity and not be able to educate people as to the importance of physical awareness.

Way Out: Connect with others and give them the gift of understanding the human body and how to nurture and care for it. As you are connected to others bodies, relay the messages their body provides through the dialogue of weight, flexibility or inflexibility, and other resources of body language.

Color Assistance:

Manifesting—Orange;
Healing—Deep Blue;
Self Power—Red.

Notes: Earl's birth date is January 20. He was born under the sign of Capricorn. The moon was in the sign of Gemini at the time of his birth and his ascendent angled at Libra. As is noted in his chart, much of the dialogue was around physical awareness. Consistently, this was brought to his attention. Capricorn is a very physical sign. It is considered to be one of the Earth elements. Researching the correlations in his chart, there was a lot of Capricorn alignment, i.e., the stone, the plant, the donkey and the healing color. (Capricorn is considered an indigo color.) His Gemini moon was also seen in his first and last name (the six in Tarot is the Lover's card, which is also associated with Gemini). Gemini is also associated with the color scheme of orange—his manifesting color. The red, though not associated to his astrological energy, is a very Earthy color. Certainly his chart represented a significant amount of Earth-type elements. His Libra ascendent was also called out in his name (the 11, which is the Justice card in Tarot and is associated with Libra) and his plant. Libra is associated to green in color which is the complementary color of red and can be seen as balancing some of his Earthy nature.

A very interesting side-note regarding this subject: At the time of his charting he was working as an accountant. Unbeknownst to this author, his background studies at a university had been in exercise physiology. He, in fact, had a Bachelor's degree in physical education. He had chosen to leave the health field after marrying in order to "make money". Once receiving his Sacred Path Wheel© he made a decision to return to the health and fitness field and complete his upper graduate studies. He indicated that he was happiest when teaching fitness or working in the health-related fields.

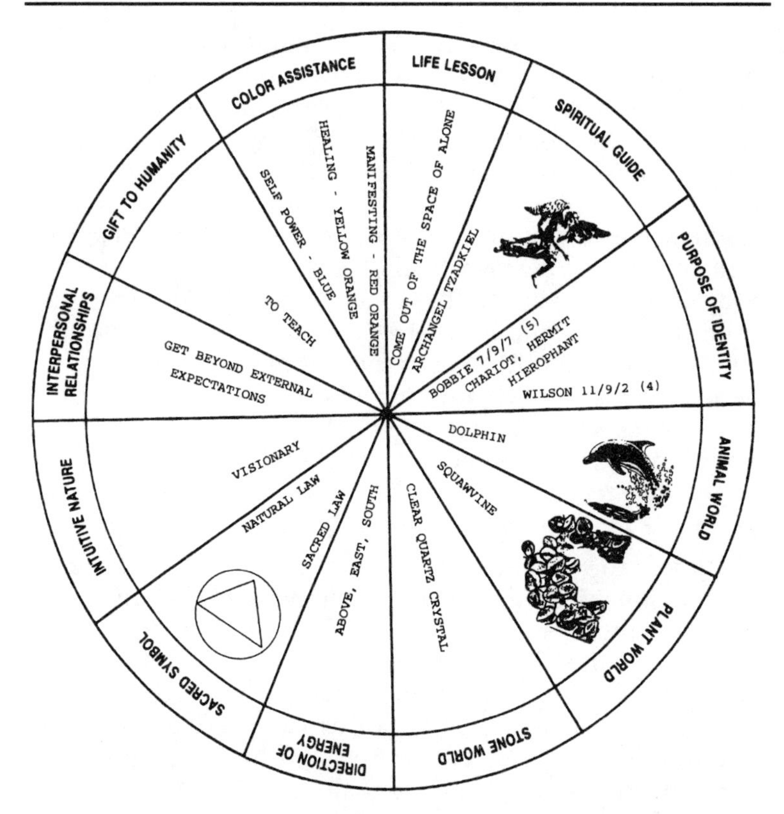

Figure 16-2
Bobbie Wilson's Sacred Path Wheel©

Reviewing the twelve spokes in her chart also proves to be an awakening to the consistent choices of one's soul.

Lesson: *Come out of the space of Alone.* This life-time is about knowing and being with others. You are not to be alone. You are to learn to accept the gift of love and honor from others. You are to associate with others; socialize; and communicate your dreams, desires, and achievements with others. Being alone is to be set aside in this life-time.

Challenge: Loneliness. While learning to achieve your lesson you may find yourself feeling lonely even in the midst of loved ones, gatherings and social situations. You may feel as though you are inside yourself and not outside

with the others. You may feel as though you are in your inner spaces with much to share, much knowledge to reveal, yet be unable to do so. Shyness will be part of this challenge. Miscommunication will occur. Sharing your own dreams, desires and achievements will feel as though they have to be "coughed up" and difficult to speak about. It will seem as though you must "hide" yourself. Rejection will be your greatest fear and experience.
Way Out: Come out of that lonely place. Be sure to gather with others. Do not allow that inner lonely separation to rule you. Come out! Accept the gift of others—a sharing, caring exploration. Communicate your needs, your dreams and desires and your achievements. Let others see the real you—and accept their acceptance. Stand up, stand out and be recognized.

Guide: *Archangel Tzadkiel*. This is an angel who will not allow you to be alone nor feel unloved. He rules the sphere of consciousness called Mercy—the place of the saints, and masters who wish to heal and help humanity. (He is also the ruler of the planet Jupiter which rules your moon sign Sagittarius.) The color of his sphere is blue—the color of your power. There are many correspondences to be seen as Tzadkiel works with you in this life time. Tzadkiel will help you know that you are not alone and that you are one of many. He compassionately assists you. He will teach you what to do to take the steps to your higher achievements. He will connect you to the Divine Light of God. He will warm your heart with inspiration, teach you to smile through adversity, to spread laughter and joy, and comfort you in your pain. He will teach you above all to love yourself and to love others.
Challenge: When not connected to Tzadkiel you will indeed feel alone on your journey through life. You will wonder if there is true compassion (especially directed toward you from others). You will have difficulty remembering what to do. You will ignore the inner prompting and be fearful in moving toward your goals. You will find you experience bigotry, hypocrisy, greed, and cruelty. You will be unable to see the bigger picture that directs your

path. You will not be able to set boundaries that support you and others. You will be scattered, confused, and mired in conflict.

Way Out: Call on Tzadkiel. Ask for his benevolent assistance. Ask that he teach you to expand your life beyond limitations and loneliness. Listen for his inner prompting and allow him to spread joy, laughter and comfort in your world. Ask him to show you how to see yourself with the many and the many with you.

Identity: *Bobbie = 7/9/7 (5); Chariot, Hermit, (Hierophant).* Each of these numbers support your life lesson as well as your gift to humanity. For your life lesson purpose let us review the meaning of these numbers. With the seven in spirit it reveals the knowing that you are guided and supported by the True Will, by the understanding of the mysteries of life, and by the ability to open the gates of this understanding and allow divine love into your present incarnation. Mentally you can carry this wisdom into a knowing for healing all past patterns of separation and loneliness by directing the mind toward its higher power. In the physical you have the ability to set boundaries that allow you to receive love, come into the space of respect and directing the pathway toward achievement of one with the many. You are at perfect choice with these numbers—you can choose to be alone or you can choose to be a part of humanity by gathering, sharing and expressing your desires, dreams and achievements. With the five in the core we recognize the inner support that provides you with strength, understanding, loving direction, and the ability to face realities, conflicts and struggles with a sense of knowing that they provide you the growth. All are teacher's numbers. All ask that you follow the path of the divine energy known as God/Goddess. To come from a state of integrity, with love, inner peace, and have the desire to serve humanity in a spiritual way.

Challenge: *Wilson = 11/9/2 (4).* Your challenges will consist of creating the balance necessary in your world to complete the projects at hand in order for you to go on to your next level. You will struggle with the sense that no

one is there to help you—that you must do it all alone. You will feel isolated and unable to communicate your needs. Rather than speak out you will become silent. Rather than have your needs met, you will see a bigger picture and the need of everyone else. However, you will have the tendency not to see yourself in this picture. You will then struggle with your physical needs, struggle with depression, and struggle with the injustice of any given situation. Periodically your world will loose its foundation and you will believe that you are going to loose everything. You will experience your "worst nightmares" and your mind will run the scenario of your greatest fears.
Way Out: Stop the activity of the negative mind. Come into the center of your being and listen to the God/Goddess within. Let the vision come clear. Focus on your desired outcome—the beauty, love, abundance, creativity, etc. that you want in the here and now. State your needs and accept the support when it is given. Recognize the loved ones that are here to support you. When you ask for something—let it come (don't ask and then wonder when; ask with a knowing that it already is.) Dream your dreams and then be ready, willing and able to act upon them. Speak with clarity so others know what you truly want (don't let them guess or try to be psychic). Ask others to speak clearly to you. Set the boundaries for the desired goals to be met. Come from love that is expansive, understanding, adaptable, and growing. Let the same come to you. Show your intelligence, your magic, your spiritual knowing—it reveals your power.

Animal: *Dolphin.* Your instinctual nature is one of higher consciousness as well. It understands how to mix with others. It is a loving nature—that also allows itself to be supported. It does not go off alone. It is always within sounding distance of a partner, loved one or large family. It is very social, playful and communicative. All of this is the supporting essence of your souls desire to achieve its life lesson. Through this fine energy you connect with the vibrations of the God/Goddess. You can dive deep within yourself for truth and the knowing of the directions you need to survive, grow, and awaken to your true power. Your instinctual nature always reminds you to breathe so you may take in the vital life force energy of the Universe.

Challenge: When not connected and listening to your instinctual nature you will drift off into separation and find yourself signaling for help—but you may be too far off the boundaries of others for them to hear or feel your needs. You will delve into the spaces of loneliness and forget the support that others can provide. You will not be sociable, playful or communicative. You will not connect to the vibrations of the God/Goddess and be directed on your course for assistance, love and healing. You will forget to breathe, slip into sorrow, experience separation, stress, and endangerment.

Way Out: Call on the nature spirit of the dolphin. Ride the waves of your instinctual nature. Let your instinctual nature connect you to the natural rhythms and flow of the Universe. Connect with others. Be sociable, supported and supportive. Communicate your need to be healed, to heal, to love and to be loved. Balance your world with play, joy, and laughter. Connect to the pure spirit within yourself and let it direct the course of your instinctual nature.

Plant: *Squawvine.* This is a plant that asks you to fulfill the need to be with others, socialize, and communicate. As a vine it grows long and intertwines itself around plants, rocks, trees and others in its pathway. It provides beautiful flowers of white and red berries for healing. It reveals that you have the ability to grow and adapt to the world around you. That you have the ability to communicate, socialize, and intertwine with others. It reveals that your adaptive, growing nature is one willing to move out into the world and connect rather than be alone. It also reveals that you have a creative nature, nurturing nature, and are able to release attitudes and experiences that no longer serve you. As a healing plant the leaves and berries are used in teas and can be used internally and externally (for sores). It is a diuretic, astringent, and uterine tonic. It helps treat bladder and vaginal infections, water retention, and diarrhea. As you use it you help keep yourself clear and balanced.

Challenge: When not aligned with the squawvine frequency you will find yourself locked in and entangled with your own self-serving ideas and attitudes. You will feel lonely, unloved and uncared for. To balance that you will have the tendency to choke out others. Your communication skills will seem lost, your socializing skills will seem inadequate, and your ability to adapt to any situation will be uncomfortable. You will hold things in, retain regrets, disappointments, and hurts. You will not feel nurtured and supported nor will you provide the same to others. Imperfections will seem to plague your world and your abilities to grow and adapt to any given situation.

Way Out: Utilize the squawvine. Plant it in your garden. Connect with it through tinctures and teas. Work with the devas of the squawvine to assist you in your growth and adaption throughout this life and through any given situation. Remember to intertwine your life with others so you may know and learn that you are not alone. Release emotions that bind you, thoughts that restrict you and fears that lock you into the realm of aloneness. Accept and allow others to support and nurture you as well as you support and nurture others.

Stone: *Clear Quartz Polished Crystal.* This stone is associated to Gemini, one of the strongest elements in your astrological chart. It does indeed show the intelligence of your soul in using this essence to bring you out of aloneness. Quartz not only calls for attention, it attracts attention. It is an energy field of magnetic attraction. It is powerful enough to generate and magnify whatever is programmed within it. Its power comes through the clarity of the mind and the spirit. It is known to amplify healing energies, strengthen your ability to connect to the True Source, and balance mental, emotional, physical and spiritual levels. It helps you to connect with and socialize, communicate and share, and be one with the many. Quartz is a very strong mineral, which of course, reveals your strength and foundation as the same.

Challenge: When not connected with this essence, you will find that you attract the negative, stressful energies of the actions of others around you. Your mind is out of focus. Your desires to achieve are unclear. Your drives are wishy-washy, and your freedom is restricted. Your foundation wobbles and the instability scares you. You then change your mind and directions erratically. No one, not even you, knows what you need and the reflections and actions of life reveal that reality (if you are able to pay attention long enough to see it). Rather than magnify power and your significant presence, you magnify negativity, frustration, and inabilities. Your imbalances keep you disconnected from True Source and True knowledge.

Way Out: Wear quartz crystal. Stay connected with its pure essence. Empower your days with the dreams of your tomorrow within your quartz. Let it magnify and attract to you the desires of your heart. Periodically clear it with meditation, rinsing under cold water, soaking in salt water, or bathing in the light of the sun and moon. See the quartz within yourself and let it be an antenna for the magnetic pull and channeling of the God/Goddess light of truth, love, power and wisdom. Let it flow through you. Keep your mind clear and focused so you may reflect the purity of your being.

Direction: Above, east and south. Entering into the Earth realm you brought the power of the divine into the clarity of your mind and the expression of your life path. All are force fields: Above, the driving force of God, east the driving element of air, and south the desire and motivating nature of fire. They reveal your inner desire to come forward on a spiritual path, be enlightened and enlighten others, experience your pathway with others, adapt, express, play and grow. It also speaks of the desire to be recognized for the intelligence and spiritual knowing that you have brought into this incarnation.

Challenge: When not connected to these directions, you may feel yourself without the drive and desire to move forward. Your mind will become unclear and unfocused, and your ability to adapt, to learn and to achieve will be challenged. Recognition will seem distant and hard work with harder work may become your reality. You may become isolated because of the hard work and need to achieve, achieve, achieve.

Way Out: Daily connect to these directional energy forces. Let them flow through you, support you and balance you. Connect with Great Spirit and listen to His/Her message for aligning to your truth for any given day. Be the clear channel for this expression. Connect to your wisdom and the strength of your mind. Maintain clear and natural mental focus. See the brightness of the sun in your life. Allow your achievements to be both hard work and joyful play. Each day acknowledge how you have connected with another—let the connection be thorough and involving all parts of yourself—your mental, emotional, physical and spiritual nature.

Symbol: *Triangle within a Circle.* You are hear to abide by Sacred Law and Natural Law. Sacred Law is the Law of laws—love. It is symbolized by the inner triangle and represents the true nature of the Universe. It encompasses all forms of existence and is nonjudgmental, constant, perfect and unchangeable. It asks that you hold all life sacred, come from your true inner core and seek the divine in all things including yourself. Natural law is depicted by the circle. It reveals the continuous expansion and contraction of the energy of this Universe. Its constant fluctuation governs your perception of time and space, cycles and phases, birth and death, involution and evolution. It reminds you to go with the flow of all things. It connects you to your intuitive nature through a strong and clear mind. It connects you with mother nature through an understanding of your own natural rhythms. It connects you with all life when you value the patterns, phases and cycles with an understanding that all is necessary in order to evolve. It asks you to understand the laws of the Universe—most particularly the Law of Cause and Effect.

Challenge: When not connected to your sacred symbol and the laws that govern it you will find that you feel disconnected from True Source, others, and stand alone on a dark and narrow pathway. You will feel like the ups and downs of life are so radical that you need the world to stop so you can get off. You will be tired—tired of the constant struggle. Your love nature will be unnurtured. You will be judgmental and be judged. You will, perhaps, be very critical of yourself. You will be unpredictable, changeable and frustrated with the erratic rhythms of your life. Physically you will find the rhythms of your body are out of balance. This will include hormonal rhythms. It will include body weight. You will also find that in the world of materialization you are trying to balance without much success. One day the money is there, the next day it is out of reach. One day the comforts of life are abundant, the next they seem as though they were just a dream. Mentally you will be clear and then unclear, struggling with decisions and always questioning, "Am I making the right decision?" In the negative you will be out of focus in your intuitive and creative visualization. You will not be connected to your spiritual vision and knowing. Emotionally this will rock you and keep you in an uncomfortable zone. It will lock up your heart space in an attempt to protect. You will wonder if you will ever connect or re-connect to the harmony and joy that you know is there for you. Spiritually, you will not be able to see the wisdom behind the events in your life.

Way Out: Honor these laws. Hold all life sacred. Come from a space and connection each day with Divine Love. Let that love flow through you and out to the world in which you encounter on a daily basis. Remember that Sacred Law is very simple—it is Love. In love there is no judgment, there is constant and perfect realities going on at all times. To honor Natural Law get in tune with the rhythms and movements of nature. Follow these rhythms. Like the Spring know when to come forward, like summer know when to act out, achieve and be recognized, at the fall time know when to sit back and reap your harvest, take in what your deserve from the action you have put out. And like the winter, know when to retreat and regenerate. Your body will speak to you about these cycles for when you are tired you will know when it is time to retreat, when you are energetic you will know when it is time to put forward efforts. When you feel urges you will know it is time to create. Learn the cycles and phases of your life. Honor them. Honor yourself and others. Honor nature. Use and understand the Laws of nature. Act in a way that the return is what you want—come from cause rather than effect. Attract through this divine law of Cause and Effect.

Your intuitive Nature: *Visionary*. When you align yourself with creative visioning you align yourself with your intuitive nature. When you are connected to your intuitive nature you see clear and precise visions. Your strength and power of your intuitive self comes through your ability to use your inner eye and your inner knowing through visualization.

Challenge: When not aligned with your intuitive nature it will be difficult for you to see with your inner eye. Then your visions of power, joy, peace, harmony, the future and even the now will be clouded. You will feel as though you cannot trust what you "see" and feel intuitively. And, indeed, you will not be able to trust what you believe is your intuitive knowing—for it will not be.

Way Out: Clear the mind of clutter, negative thinking, and unfocused direction. Take the time to focus on clear and precise visions. Then allow yourself to release this vision to your God/Goddess within. Await the inner stirring of your intuitive power to direct the vision of your now, your future and your knowing. Then act upon it.

Relationships: *Get beyond external expectations.* As you act and interact with others throughout this life-time, you are to connect with their wholeself and you are to allow others to connect with your wholeself. It is done without expectation. It is done through a willingness to share, to express your needs and your boundaries, and with a willingness to adapt when necessary. This will allow you and others to connect with a true and loving inner nature. Nothing external will provide a true relationship and learning about others in this life. It will only keep you separated and lonely, for your Inner Being will know there is more. Get beyond expectations that are only surface needs.

Challenge: Expectations that cannot be served will become your nemesis. You will expect too much. You will experience discontentment and disconnection with others. You will not feel wanted or a part of the interrelationships in your surroundings. Relationships will not support your growth and life lesson and you will become scattered and challenged. Setbacks will occur that leave you feeling uncared for and alone.

Way Out: Expect nothing and accept everything. Be willing to share who you are, some of the mysteries of yourself and others, and connect with others from their inner spaces to their outer reality. Know that outer expectations are unreal and nonsupportive. Initiate new ways to relate to others that bring out their true inner self, and not just the surface information.

Gift: *To teach.* Give your gift to others in the form of teaching. Teach what you know and what you connect to in the power of your spiritual nature, through the clarity of your mind, and the focus of your truth. Show others how to delve deep within themselves and create transformations that can free them. Expand on the truths and the wisdom of the Universe as you see it and can share it. Come from your space of joy, love and care.

Challenge: When not teaching and gifting to humanity you will find that you feel contracted into the darkness and secrets of the Universe. You will feel as though you need recognition but are not receiving it. You will be frustrated in your inability to transform your own life and bring yourself into the state of freedom. You will be stuck in the loftiness of the Universal ozone trying to figure out how you are to come forward with truth knowledge, joy and recognition. You will not be able to ground and manifest what you know.

Way Out: Teach. Stand up and be recognized. You already know from within that you are a loving, caring person. You already know that you have much to share along the lines of wisdom, self transformation, intuitive knowing, and the wisdom of the ages. Utilize the strength of your mind, your ability to communicate, and your joy in sharing and associating with others. Discipline your life to allow your teaching.

Color:

Manifesting—Red Orange;
Healing—Yellow orange;
Self Power—Blue.

Notes: Bobbie's theme was constantly repeated—to be with others, to not be alone. Every element in her wheel supports togetherness. Even in her gift to humanity she is asked to be amongst people as a teacher.

What becomes apparent after review of several wheels is the constant interlinking of information from spoke-to-spoke. Colors, messages of animals, plants and minerals, the elements of Fire, Water, Air and Earth, all interconnect and enhance the energy for achievement of the goal. Repeatedly, associations are seen from spoke-to-spoke and the intelligence of the soul becomes evident.

Each person receiving a Sacred Path Wheel© also receives a cassette recording of the wheel and other information provided by the Spirit realm. Often past lives are released to reveal the reason why the life lesson was chosen for the present incarnation. Not only do the past lives reveal why the lesson, but also, in many cases, reveals why a certain interpersonal relationship power is being directed into this life, or why a particular law was left out. Incredibly, the soul provides the wisdom for every choice made and seen within the Sacred Path Wheel©.

The Soul Is Magical

Through review of all Sacred Path Wheels an understanding of choice becomes evident. Each individual soul assesses the life to be experienced and prepares to walk through a path of physical living toward a purpose. It is aware of what frequencies of the Universe it must use in order to create the field of existence that will provide the greatest magnetic pull toward achieving the life lesson. The soul gathers these frequencies as though pulling ribbons of energies from the Universe and channels them into matter and experiences on the Earth. These ribbons, when integrated into matter take on the form of the personality and supporting essences (such as people, circumstances, and events). As seen in the instinctual nature, growth nature, and nature for providing strength, power and foundation, these frequencies appear as animals, plants or minerals. In fact, if not chosen for personal use through a human consciousness, those frequencies would be used as an animal, plant, or mineral on the Earth. The supporting energies of the cosmos (sun, moon, stars and planets) at the time of birth are additional frequencies used to establish patterns for achievement of a life lesson. Such use of choice establishes an intelligence beyond human conditioning. It is the *MAGIC OF THE SOUL.*

BIBLIOGRAPHY

Andrews, Ted (1993)
Animal-Speak
St. Paul, MN: Llewellyn Publications

Atwood, Mary Dean (1991)
Spirit Healing
New York, NY: Sterling Publishing Company Inc.

Bear, Sun, et al. (1991)
Dancing With The Wheel, The Medicine Wheel Work Book
New York, NY: Prentice Hall Press

Bletzer, Ph.D., June G. (1987)
The Donning International Encyclopedic Psychic Dictionary
Norfolk, VA: The Donning Company/Publishers

Bopp, Julie, et al. (1985)
The Sacred Tree
Wilmut, WI: Lotus Light

Cunningham, Scott (1991)
Cunningham's Encyclopedia of Magical Herbs
St. Paul, MN: Llewellyn Publishers

Davidson, Gustav (1971)
A Dictionary of Angels Including the Fallen Angels
New York, NY: Free Press

Fortune, Dion (1989)
The Mystical Qabalah
York Beach, ME: Samuel Weiser, Inc.

Gerber, M.D., Richard (1988)
Vibrational Medicine
Santa Fe, NM: Bear & Company

Glass-Koentop, Pattalee (1991)
Year of Moons, Seasons of Trees
St. Paul, MN: Llewellyn Publishers

Godwin, Malcolm (1990)
Angels, An Endangered Species
New York, NY: Simon and Schuster

Gonzalez-Wippler, Migene (1987)
A Kabbalah For the Modern World
St. Paul, MN: Llewellyn Publishers

Gray, William G. (1987)
The Ladder of Lights
York Beach, ME: Samuel Weiser, Inc.

GURUDAS (1983)
Flower Essences and Vibrational Healing
Albuquerque, NM: Brotherhood of Life, Inc.

GURUDAS (1985)
Gem Elixirs and Vibrational Healing, Vol. 1
Boulder, CO: Cassandra Press

Haich, Elisabeth (1974)
Initiation
Palo Alto, CA: Seed Center

Hall, Manly P. (1958)
Astrological Keywords
Savage, MD: Littlefield Adams Quality Paperbacks

Hall, Manly P. (1977)
The Secret Teachings of All Ages
Los Angeles, CA: The Philosophical Research Society, Inc.

Hawk, Medicine & Cat, Grey (1990)
American Indian Ceremonies
New Brunswick, NJ: Inner Light Publications

Holmes, Ernest (1966)
The Science of Mind
New York, NY: G. P. Putnam's Sons

Hopman, Ellen Evert (1992)
Tree Medicine, Tree Magic
Custer, WA: Phoenix Publishing, Inc.

Huntley, Janis (1990)
The Elements of Astrology
Great Britain: Element Books Limited

Hutchens, Alma R. (1986)
Indian Herbology of North America
Windsor 14, Ontario, Canada: MERCO

Kautz, William H., & Branon, Melanie (1987)
Channeling, The Intuitive Connection
San Francisco, CA: Harper & Row

Klimo, Jon (1987)
Channeling: Investigations on Receiving Information From Paranormal Sources
Los Angeles, CA: Jeremy P. Tarcher, Inc.

Lamsa, George M. (1968)
Holy Bible
From the Ancient Eastern Text
New York, NY: Harper & Row, Publishers

March, Marion D., & McEvers, Joan (1989)
The Only Way To Learn Astrology, Vol. 1
San Diego, CA: ACS Publications, Inc.

Matthews, John (1991)
The Celtic Shaman
Great Britain: Element Books Limited

Melia, Dorothee L. (1986)
Stone Power
New York, NY: Warner Books, Inc.

Moolenburgh, H.C. (1990)
A Handbook of Angels
Great Britain: Hillman Prints, Ltd.

Mowrey, Ph.D., Daniel B. (1986)
The Scientific Validation of Herbal Medicine
New Canaan, CT: Keats Publishing, Inc.

Parrinder, Geoffrey (1983)
World Religions From Ancient History to the Present
New York, NY: Facts On File

Pollack, Rachel (1980)
Seventy-Eight Degrees of Wisdom (A book of Tarot, Part 1: The Major Arcana)
Great Britain: The Aquarian Press

Raphaell, Katerina (1986)
Crystal Enlightenment, Vol. 1
New York, NY: Aurora Press

Sams, Jamie, & Carson, David (1988)
Medicine Cards: The Discovery of Power Through The Ways of Animals
Santa Fe, NM: Bear & Company

Sullivan, Kevin (1987)
The Crystal Handbook
New York, NY: Signet

Thorsten, Geraldine (1989)
The Goddess In Your Stars
New York, NY: Simon & Schuster, Inc.

Tierra, C.A., N.D., Michael (1980)
The Way of Herbs
New York, NY: Pocket Books

Tiffen, Greg (1987)
General Numerological Aspects
San Diego, CA: KAIROS Institute

Torres Msc.D., Ph.D., Katherine (1994)
Stone Spirit Calling
Carlsbad, CA: Earth People Medicine

Tredennick, Hugh (1982)
Plato, The Last Days of Socrates
New York, NY: Penguin Books

Zalewski, C.L. (1990)
Herbs In Magic and Alchemy
New York, NY: Avery Publishing

Sacred Path Wheel©
Training & Certification

Are you one of the many individuals aligned with intuitive abilities? Are you interested in being certified as someone who can amass the energy of a Soul Journey and chart a *Sacred Path Wheel©*, the unseen energy of soul magic?

Twice yearly (in May and October) Dr. Torres offers a week-long intensive for the study and certification of those interested in charting the journey of soul intelligence.

Participants are trained to work with the spiritual counsel of the *Sacred Path Wheel©* and the correlating factors affecting individual pathways.

This training is designed exclusively for individuals who want to bring healing into their practice for others. Those in training must have intuitive background and be a practitioner of intuitive counseling.

Enrollment is limited to assure close communication between teacher and student. Each individual must obtain their own transportation and hotel accommodations.

A four-page letter describing yourself and your interest as a *Sacred Path Wheel©* counselor is required.

Please forward your interest to:

Dr. Katherine Torres
P.O. Box 597
San Marcos, CA 92079-0597

Dr. Torres is also available to travel to your center for this training.

ABOUT THE AUTHOR

Katherine Torres, Ph.D. holds degrees in Metaphysical Sciences and Transpersonal Psychology. She practices Shamanistic methods of her Celtic ancestry as well as the natives of the Great Americas to receive information from the Sacred Path of life. She journeys into the inner realms and retrieves the knowledge necessary to produce a 12-spoke wheel. As she shape-shifts, the information becomes clear and the translation easy.

Dr. Torres began her quest for knowledge of this vast Universe after a mystical experience occurred in her late teens. It reconfirmed her childhood experiences with Spirit and sent her questioning religious authorities. When none could provide answers to the knowledge swimming within, she sought the study of mysticism for insight. The gift of this study and the connection with spirit has fulfilled her drive to personally know God/Goddess—the Creator of All Life. She has, for the past 30-plus years, shared this knowledge with others through the intuitive arts. After the death of her father in 1983, she began a communication with an entity, Malachi, that has expanded her spiritual knowledge even further. Through this connection she has been able to reconnect to her ancestral knowledge, channel Universal information, and provide insights to others.

Dr. Torres has a full-time practice in San Diego, California where she counsels, teaches, and performs sacred ceremonies for healing the personal self and the world. She is the founder and president of The Center For Spiritual Advancement. Her spare time is spent writing, joining the activities of her husband, family of six children and eight grandchildren, and spending sacred time in nature.

Forthcoming books by Dr. Torres include: a Tarot workbook and deck, *Archetypal Numerology, WomanSpirit*, a series of workshops on cassette for connecting with the Divine Feminine Essence, and a book with cards revealing her journeys with the moon mothers.

Ordering Your
Sacred Path Wheel©

The *Sacred Path Wheel*© maps the intelligence of your soul. It reveals the energy your soul accesses to follow the purpose of its lesson. This energy is your alliance with spiritual guidance, instinctive and intuitive knowing, and your ability to adapt and grow. Further, your soul accesses the treasure of relating to others. As you progress to higher levels of your inner truth, you radiate and access the lights of healing, manifesting the power of your Self. This keeps you in balance with the Universal Laws you follow throughout your life.

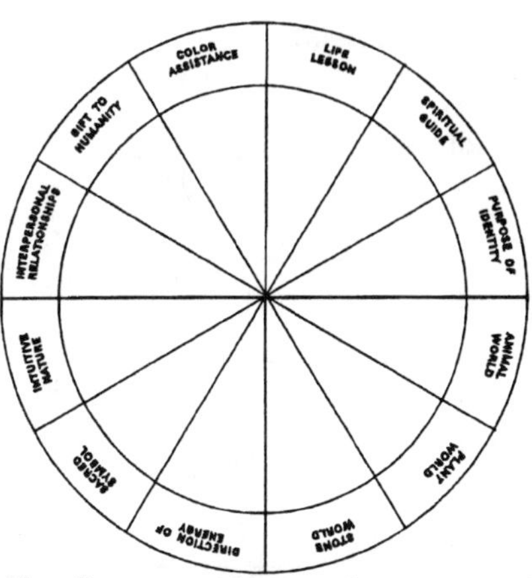

> *"In the challenges of life, the Sacred Path Wheel provides the direction I need when I'm feeling out of balance. In addition to pointing to the path of my life lesson, the Wheel offers ways to stay on that path during physical, mental and spiritual challenges. It's an excellent guide for leading a balanced and fulfilling life."*
> —*Michelle Adams*

> *"I would like to acknowledge the self-empowering process I experienced after receiving my Sacred Path Wheel. Each part of the Wheel reveals a part of myself that I embrace wholly."*
> —*Llizane Schmidt*

> *"Wonderful! Opened so much knowledge of myself to my awareness. Had it done for my whole family..."*
> —*Joanne Demby*

You may have your own *SOUL MAGIC* revealed. A Sacred Path Wheel may be ordered by filling in the form on the next page.

Sacred Path Wheel© Order Form

Name: ____
first middle last

Other Name(s): ______________________________________
e.g., maiden name, nicknames, etc.

Address: ____
street address

____
city state/province zip/postal code

____
country

Date/time of birth: ___________________________________
month day year time

Place of birth: ______________________________________
city state/province country

If this a gift check the appropriate box and fill in the lines below:

❒ Christmas ❒ Birthday ❒ Relationships ❒ Other ________

Your Name: ____
first middle last

Your Address: _______________________________________
street address

____
city state/province zip/postal code

For each *Sacred Path Wheel,* audio cassette and written report, send a copy of this form and $150.00 in U.S. funds to:

Metaphysical Counseling Group
P.O. Box 597
San Marcos, CA 92079-0579
Telephone: (619) 546-2398

Please allow 3 to 6 weeks for delivery.